bs.

The Good
Manager's
Guide

The **Good Manager's Guide**

Over 130 practical checklists for day-to-day management

Trevor Boutall

MCI, Russell House, 10-12 Russell Square, London WC1B 5BZ
Telephone: 0171 872 9000
Facsimile: 0171 872 9099
Website: http://www.bbi.co.uk/mci
E-mail: nfmed_mci@compuserve.com

Registered Charity No. 1002554

Management Charter Initiative is the operating arm of the
National Forum for Management Education and Development.

First edition 1994
Second edition 1997

ISBN 1 897587 80 5

Printed and bound in Great Britain by
Creative Print and Design Wales, Ebbw Vale

The publication of the **Good Manager's Guide** was warmly welcomed by managers seeking to understand their responsibilities and looking for practical ways to improve their performance at work. Although the guide was designed as a set of checklists for practising managers, feedback suggests that it has been put to a variety of other uses, including

- defining job roles for managers
- specifying the performance and skills required of managers
- drafting job descriptions and recruitment advertisements
- identifying and prioritising training needs
- drafting personal development plans
- preparing and delivering training programmes and workshops
- planning and monitoring continuing professional development
- setting performance objectives and appraising performance.

The **Good Manager's Guide** has been extensively used by managers in the UK in private, public and voluntary organisations. Special editions have been produced for organisations as diverse as the Labour Party and the Law Society. It has also been translated into several languages, including Chinese.

The guide has been well received but people have asked for improvements. In particular, they wanted more extensive coverage of specialist areas of management such as

- marketing
- quality
- environmental issues
- energy
- purchasing
- finance
- personnel planning
- project management
- information and communication systems.

This second edition includes an additional fifty-four checklists, comprehensively addressing all these areas. The original checklists have also been fully updated to reflect recent trends and developments in best practice in management as described in the new Management Standards. For those organisations which are using the Management Standards, and for individuals who are working towards National Vocational Qualifications or Scottish Vocational Qualifications, the checklists and the standards are also clearly cross-referenced in Appendix 1.

Good management is about enabling people to perform to their highest potential. I trust this book will do just that. Good management is also about continuous improvement. This second edition is a major enhancement of the first, building on its strengths and responding to feedback from users. I hope readers will continue to give me feedback, so I can ensure that the **Good Manager's Guide** continues to have a visible impact on management performance for many years to come.

Trevor Boutall
September, 1997

Contents

How to use this guide

The manager's role is complex. Managers are often required to perform a number of functions simultaneously, drawing on a wide repertoire of skills and a broad suite of technical and specialist knowledge as well as common sense. They are required to respond to fast-changing circumstances and work at many different levels.

To many managers, the job of management remains a mystery, a journey in a foreign land full of the terrors of the unknown. This guide seeks to chart that territory and to show that, although the problem may be complex, the answer is often simple.

The **Good Manager's Guide** breaks the management role down into simple, practical checklists to help you tackle everyday tasks successfully. There is no magic in it, just crystal clear objectives and strictly logical steps.

The checklists can be used for a variety of purposes, such as job descriptions, recruitment, appraisal schemes and performance management. However, they are designed, first and foremost, to help you do your job. Here are some examples of how you might use them.

Addressing unfamiliar tasks

You may be faced with a task you have not performed for a long time, or perhaps never met before. Take recruiting a new team member for example. How would you go about it?

The contents page tells you that, under **Manage people**, there is a section on **Personnel planning**. There are five checklists to help you. **Planning human resource requirements** will help you check whether recruitment is the best option at this stage. **Drawing up job specifications** will help you clarify what the job entails and the sort of person who would be suitable. **Attracting the right candidates** provides guidance on how to advertise. **Assessing and selecting team members** will give you guidance on how to choose the right person for the job and **Appointing team members** will ensure you meet all the organisational and legal requirements.

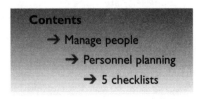

Contents

→ Manage people

→ Personnel planning

→ 5 checklists

Tackling important tasks

You may have to do something critically important which you want to ensure you get right – running an important meeting for instance.

The index at the back of the book points you to the checklist for **Leading** *meetings*. This will help to ensure you get the best from all partici-pants, arrive at well-informed deci-sions and get there in the fastest possible time.

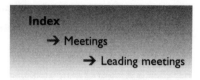

Index
→ Meetings
→ Leading meetings

Checking that you are doing things properly

Preparing budgets for your plans and projects may be something you do on a regular basis but you may like to check occasionally that you are doing things properly.

Contents
→ Manage resources
→ Managing budgets
→ Preparing budgets

The contents page shows there is a section on budgets under **Manage Resources**, with a checklist specifi-cally for **Preparing budgets**. There are also useful checklists to help you negotiate, agree and monitor your budgets.

Carrying out a public task

Some aspects of management are more public than others, so it is impor-tant not just to get it right, but to be seen to get it right.

For example, **Defining your organ-isation's mission** involves consul-tation and discussion with all your stakeholders, and needs careful negotiation to ensure it attracts the widest possible support.

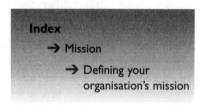

Index
→ Mission
→ Defining your organisation's mission

You should find checklists to cover all your management tasks, though they may not cover all your specialist functions. They are based on the national Management Standards, developed by the Management Charter Initiative (MCI).

Using the checklists for personal development

You may wish to use the checklists in a more structured way to support your personal and career development as a manager. To do this, follow these simple steps.

Step 1   What are the new or challenging management issues you will be facing in the next 6-12 months?

Step 2   What are your career plans, and what new management experi-ences will you need to have to achieve these plans?

Step 3   Prioritise the five most important and urgent management issues and experiences identified in steps 1 and 2.

Step 4   Using the contents pages or the index in this guide, identify the checklists which will help you.

Step 5   Plan any development activities or training you need to gain the knowledge and skills in order to carry out these activities effectively.

Step 6   Undertake your training and development and carry out these activities according to the checklists.

Step 7   Assess your own performance – did you follow the checklists? – and ask others to give you feedback.

Use checklist 37 **Developing your skills** to help you with this.

If you can show that your performance meets the standard described in the checklists, you could qualify for a National Vocational Qualification or Scottish Vocational Qualification in Management. Refer to Appendix 1 for more details.

PART I

Operational management

The key purpose of management is to achieve the organisation's objectives and continuously improve its performance.

Operational management is being clear about the objectives you have to achieve through your team, in your department or for your part of the business; and using the available resources to best effect.

It involves managing the operation of your part of the organisation as effectively as possible; being clear about what you are expected to deliver; designing systems and procedures; and organising the workplace to achieve this. You always need to be looking for, and implementing, ways of doing things better to provide a quality service or product every time.

Operational management means getting things done through people. You have to make sure you have the right people to do the job. You have to develop a team and help each member of the team develop the skills they need to perform their job effectively. You need to plan the work and allocate it amongst the team, setting individual objectives and providing feedback on their performance. Managing people involves building effective working relationships and dealing with difficult problems, being careful to be fair and equitable in all your dealings.

As a manager, you will often be required to prepare budgets for the expenditure, and perhaps income, for your part of the operation. It is your responsibility to ensure that these financial targets are met and that all team members are aware of how they can help in improving the financial performance. *Operational management* also involves obtaining and using information to aid decision-making; and leading and participating effectively in meetings to arrive at decisions.

Operational management is a complex business requiring a range of skills and knowledge, together with disciplined time management, if you are to succeed. However, the checklists in this book provide some simple, practical guidelines for effectively tackling everyday tasks. You will find them relevant whether you are a team leader, supervisor or manager at any level, although you may find your role is to contribute to, rather than to have full responsibility for, an activity.

1 Manage activities

Meeting customer needs
Marketing
Managing change
Project management
Quality assurance
Environmental management

2 Manage people

Managing yourself
Personnel planning
Developing teams and individuals
Managing teams and individuals
Working relationships
Managing problems with your team
Equal opportunities

3 Manage resources

Managing physical resources
Managing budgets
Controlling finances
Selecting suppliers
Contracting for supply
Managing energy

4 Manage information

Establishing information management
    and communication systems
Using information
Meetings

CHAPTER 1

Manage activities

Manage activities is about working out ways of meeting customer requirements on time, every time.

Meeting customer needs

This section is about maintaining an effective operation to meet customer needs.

The checklists will help you to

- be clear about the needs of your customers
- plan to meet those needs
- ensure suppliers provide value for money
- maintain a safe and efficient working environment
- design your operational systems to meet customer specifications
- solve problems for customers when things go wrong.

The process of *Meeting customer needs* looks like this.

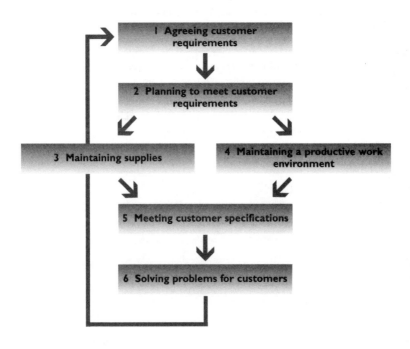

Agreeing customer requirements

❑ **Research your customers' needs** – use formal and informal techniques to identify the services or products your customers, or potential customers, need.

❑ **Design your services or products to meet your customers' needs** – and ensure your services and products meet legal and organisational requirements and resource constraints.

❑ **Describe your services or products clearly** – explain your services or products to customers, think about the person you are talking to, and make sure you communicate in a manner and at a pace which is appropriate.

❑ **Encourage customers to discuss their requirements** – invite them to seek clarification wherever appropriate and tell you how well you are meeting their needs.

❑ **Communicate frequently with customers** – develop a relationship of trust and goodwill, and keep them informed about any changes which affect them.

❑ **Ensure agreements meet legal and organisational requirements** – consult specialists if you are in doubt.

❑ **Negotiate effectively** – use your experience of past negotiations to ensure the success of future negotiations.

❑ **Optimise agreements** – create a win-win situation, where you achieve your objectives whilst meeting customer needs.

❑ **Draw up detailed specifications** – ensure that specifications of customised services or products contain all the relevant information to allow customer requirements to be met.

❑ **Keep accurate records** – include all relevant information about customer agreements.

Planning to meet customer requirements

- ❏ **Involve relevant people in the planning –** get team members, colleagues, specialists, even customers themselves to help you plan your activities.

- ❏ **Draw on experience –** use information about past successes and failures to prepare your plans.

- ❏ **Plan for contingencies –** what is likely to change in the future? Make sure your plans can cope with potential changes in circumstances.

- ❏ **Develop realistic plans –** will they meet customer requirements within the agreed timescales?

- ❏ **Develop consistent plans –** are they consistent with your organisation's objectives, resources and policies, and with legal requirements?

- ❏ **Design customer-focused operations –** organise all your operations to provide the most efficient service to your customers.

- ❏ **Discuss your plans –** check that all involved understand their role in the plans and are committed to making them work.

- ❏ **Promote helpful attitudes –** encourage members of your team to put the customers first and to take personal responsibility for meeting customer needs.

Maintaining supplies

❏ **Identify the supplies you need** – check they are sufficient to meet customer requirements.

❏ **Identify and develop suitable sources of supply** – make sure your suppliers can provide you with the materials you need for your product and services; always have alternative suppliers available for contingencies, if possible.

❏ **Select suppliers objectively** – apply fair criteria in choosing your suppliers.

❏ **Negotiate effectively** – make sure you get the best value for money and quality of service consistent with your organisation's values.

❏ **Keep complete and accurate records of negotiations and agreements with suppliers** – and pass this information on to appropriate people as soon as possible.

❏ **Maintain goodwill** – throughout your negotiations with suppliers, make sure you retain their goodwill, and find mutually acceptable ways of settling any disputes.

❏ **Review your suppliers regularly** – check they continue to offer best value for money and quality of service.

❏ **Keep accurate records of suppliers and supplies** – keep a complete list of suppliers' details and monitor levels of supplies regularly.

❏ **Watch market and economic trends which may affect supplies** – keep an eye on factors such as raw materials, cost/availability, competitor activity or changes to legislation which may affect the price or availability of supplies.

❏ **Take action where there are likely to be problems or opportunities with supplies** – where your information suggests changes to supplies which may give you problems or opportunities, take, or recommend, appropriate action to turn the situation to your advantage.

Maintaining a productive work environment

- ❑ **Ensure the environment is as conducive to work as possible –** involve your team members in assessing the work environment to see if there are different ways it could be arranged to improve productivity.

- ❑ **Ensure that conditions satisfy legal and organisational requirements –** check the relevant legislation and your internal guidelines, and make sure you have a safe work environment.

- ❑ **Provide information and support –** make sure your team members are aware of their responsibilities under health and safety legislation and that they receive any necessary training and support.

- ❑ **Cater for special needs –** provide for any special needs of employees or potential employees to ensure they can work productively.

- ❑ **Make sure equipment is properly maintained and used only by competent personnel –** regularly check all equipment in your area to see that it is properly maintained and that relevant people have been trained to use it.

- ❑ **Ensure you have a sufficient supply of resources –** plan what materials, equipment and resources you require to keep your operation running smoothly.

- ❑ **Where you do not have sufficient resources, refer to the appropriate people –** let them know immediately if you are likely to run out of anything.

- ❑ **Pass on recommendations for improving conditions –** where you identify opportunities for improving working conditions, let the appropriate people know right away, so the organisation can benefit as soon as possible.

- ❑ **Report accidents and incidents promptly and accurately –** check that you, and your team members, are fully aware of the accident and hazard procedures and that they are followed at all times.

- ❑ **Keep accurate records –** make sure your department's maintenance and health and safety records are accurate, legible and up-to-date.

5   Meeting customer specifications

❏ **Check that specifications are clear, complete and accurate –** where there is any omission or ambiguity, get clarification from your customer.

❏ **Draw up plans and schedules to meet these specifications –** allow for contingencies in these plans.

❏ **Brief all relevant people –** make sure they understand how the specifications, plans and schedules affect them.

❏ **Monitor activities, services and products –** monitor what is happening and take appropriate action to ensure specifications are met.

❏ **Make best use of resources –** use your human, capital and financial resources efficiently to meet the specifications.

❏ **Encourage individuals to take responsibility for meeting customer requirements –** involve members of your team in finding the best way to meet specifications and gain their commitment.

❏ **Give people feedback and training –** tell them how well they are doing in meeting customer requirements and give them any training necessary.

❏ **Get feedback from customers –** use this feedback to improve future operations.

❏ **Minimise disruptions to operations –** take appropriate action to reduce any factors which may disrupt operations.

❏ **Take corrective action –** implement any changes without delay and inform relevant team members, colleagues and customers about these.

❏ **Monitor corrective action –** make sure that changes are working, and use this experience to improve future operations.

❏ **Keep complete and accurate records of operations –** keep records of activities and how well you met customer specifications and make these records available to appropriate people.

Solving problems for customers 6

- ❑ **Design systems to anticipate and avoid problems for customers** – design all your procedures to meet customer needs.

- ❑ **Advise customers about your policies and procedures for solving their problems** – use appropriate media to publish your policies, procedures and alternative sources of assistance to which customers may refer.

- ❑ **Identify and acknowledge the customer's perception of the problem** – where problems do occur, listen carefully in order to understand and acknowledge the customer's view of the problem.

- ❑ **Gather all information relevant to the customer's problem** – refer to records and other people involved in order to get a full picture of the problem.

- ❑ **Summarise the customer's problem** – summarise their perceptions and all other relevant information and check that the customer agrees with your summary of the problem.

- ❑ **Keep the customer informed** – tell the customer how you plan to resolve the problem, how long it will take and give the customer progress reports where appropriate.

- ❑ **Refer to organisational procedures** – examine and interpret procedures for handling customer complaints to identify a solution.

- ❑ **Seek advice from colleagues or senior managers** – where organisational procedures do not offer a satisfactory solution ask colleagues for help in identifying alternative solutions.

- ❑ **Implement the solution promptly** – once the solution has been identified, take prompt action to solve the customer's problem and inform the customer of the action taken.

- ❑ **Monitor the delivery of the solution** – and make appropriate modifications to resolve any problems arising.

- ❑ **Check customer's satisfaction** – where appropriate, check that the problem has been solved to the customer's satisfaction.

- ❑ **Develop new procedures** – review the process and where policies or procedures do not offer a satisfactory solution, revise or develop new policies or procedures to avoid or address similar situations.

→ Marketing

This section is about anticipating, stimulating and satisfying the needs of your customers in a cost-effective way.

The checklists will help you to

- decide what market you are in
- develop a marketing plan to match the capabilities of your organisation to the needs of your customers
- develop products and services to meet your customers' needs
- decide how you price your products and services and how you deliver them to your customers
- develop plans to communicate with your customers and sell your products and services
- evaluate how successful you are in meeting your marketing objectives.

The process for **Marketing** looks like this.

7 | Developing your markets

❑ **Get up-to-date information about your markets –** use formal techniques such as market research and tracking studies as well as informal discussions with colleagues, field staff, customers and suppliers to get accurate information on current and potential markets.

❑ **Identify opportunities –** analyse the information to assess trends and developments and spot market opportunities.

❑ **Consult with colleagues –** discuss opportunities with colleagues to get a fuller picture of the impact of these opportunities on your organisation.

❑ **Evaluate opportunities –** what are the potential benefits for your organisation? What are the pros and cons of different opportunities?

❑ **Check for consistency –** do the market opportunities fit well with your organisation's mission, objectives and policies? Are they consistent with your organisation's current activities and market position?

❑ **Define your objectives –** your objectives to develop markets should be SMART

  • Specific
  • Measurable
  • Achievable and Agreed
  • Realistic
  • Time-bound.

❑ **Make clear recommendations to develop markets –** present your recommendations clearly to the relevant people in your organisation together with supporting information and a well-argued case.

❑ **Develop your markets –** if your recommendations are approved, develop and implement your marketing plan.

Developing a marketing plan

❏ **Get people involved** – encourage appropriate colleagues and members of your team to contribute to the development of your marketing plan.

❏ **Marshall the necessary information** – make sure you have all the necessary marketing research information to hand and that it is up-to-date and accurate.

❏ **Assess the environment** – use the available information to make an accurate appraisal of the opportunities and threats in the external environment and the strengths and weaknesses of your own organisation.

❏ **Define your key marketing objectives** – make sure these are SMART.

- Specific
- Measurable
- Achievable and Agreed
- Realistic
- Time-bound

and make sure they are consistent with your organisation's mission, objectives and policy.

❏ **Identify relevant components of the marketing mix** – specify your products and services, distribution and sales channels, pricing policy and communications strategy; ensure detailed plans for each of these components are prepared.

❏ **Forecast income** – make realistic assessments of the expected value and volume of sales and other income.

❏ **Forecast expenditure and resources required** – make realistic assessments of the financial, human and capital resources required to achieve your plan.

❏ **Prepare an income and expenditure budget** – include a statement of the assumptions made, the risks involved and the contingencies allowed for.

❏ **Present your marketing plan** – present the plan

- in a form which helps decision-makers to make an 'approval' decision, and
- in a way which reflects the commitment of those who will be involved in its implementation.

❏ **Implement your marketing plan** – and monitor its effects.

Developing new products and services

❑ **Generate ideas for new products and services** – encourage relevant colleagues, team members and outsiders to come up with ideas which could be of interest to the organisation.

❑ **Identify new products and services with market potential** – check whether there is a viable market and what its value might be.

❑ **Prioritise** – make a short list of those products and services which are the most suitable for your organisation's objectives, needs and capabilities.

❑ **Develop a full product or service concept for each shortlisted product or service** – outline its market, features, benefits, costs, price, distribution channels and potential sales.

❑ **Prepare the business case** – this should include

- a description of the product or service
- a description of the market, and how the product or service meets a specific need
- how it fits with your organisation's mission, objectives and policies
- how it fits with your organisation's other products, services and activities
- an estimate of expenditure, broken down into development costs, promotional costs and production/delivery costs
- an estimate of income, including pricing/discounting strategy, sales volumes and value
- the net benefits over time
- a statement of the assumptions made, dependencies, risks and contingencies allowed for
- an assessment against selection criteria (such as gross margin, profitability, total sales value, unit price or return on investment)

❑ **Present the business case** – present your proposal

- in a form which helps decision-makers to make an 'approval' decision, and
- in a way which reflects the commitment of those who will be involved in developing and marketing the new product or service.

❑ **Develop the new product or service** – if your proposal is approved, plan and develop the new product or service within the agreed time, resource and quality constraints.

❑ **Feedback positively to those involved** – if your proposal is not approved, tell those who were involved in generating or developing the idea in a way that keeps them motivated.

Determining a pricing strategy　　　　10

- ❑ **Get people involved** – encourage appropriate colleagues and members of your team to contribute to the development of your pricing strategy.
- ❑ **Marshall the necessary information** – make sure you have relevant, up-to-date pricing information to hand, including information on competitors and potential competitors.
- ❑ **Estimate the effects of alternative pricing strategies** – take into account likely effects on
  - customers, distributors and competitors – how will they react?
  - margins – will the margin be sufficient to meet your organisation's objectives?
  - other products and services – what will be the impact on prices and sales of the rest of your range?
  - product and service life cycle – are you trying to extend the life of your product or service, or speed up its progress to maturity?
  - legislative requirements – what are the legal constraints on your pricing strategy?
  - discounting and payment policies – do these need to be adjusted in the light of new pricing strategies?
- ❑ **Present your pricing plan** – include in your plan
  - the argued case for your recommended strategy
  - a summary of its likely effects
  - an analysis of costs and benefits
  - how it fits with your organisation's objectives
  - a detailed implementation plan identifying tasks and responsibilities, resources required, time scales, budgets and controls.
- ❑ **Communicate your pricing plan** – when your plan has been approved, make sure all those involved or affected are aware of its implications and their responsibilities.
- ❑ **Implement your pricing strategy** – and monitor its effects.
- ❑ **Review your pricing strategy** – review your strategy regularly and in response to changes in business performance, market and economic conditions.

11 | Deciding on distribution methods

❏ **Get people involved** – encourage appropriate colleagues, members of your team, customers and intermediaries to contribute to your decisions on distribution methods.

❏ **Marshall the necessary information** – make sure you have relevant, up-to-date information to hand including information on distribution methods used by competitors and potential competitors.

❏ **Define criteria for assessing distribution methods** – decide on which features are critical to successful distribution, and which other features would be desirable.

❏ **Analyse alternative distribution channels and methods** – consider costs, risks, returns of damaged or unwanted products, customer service requirements and customer perceptions of alternative methods.

❏ **Consider the logistics of alternative channels and methods** – what are the implications for packaging, storage, warehousing, transportation, delivery, receipt by customer?

❏ **Assess alternative distribution channels and methods** – identify the channel and method which best meets the criteria you have defined.

❏ **Present your distribution plan** – present your detailed plan, including strategy, objectives, logistics, tasks and responsibilities, resources required, time scales, budgets and controls.

❏ **Communicate your distribution plan** – when your plan has been approved, make sure all those involved or affected are aware of its implications and their responsibilities.

❏ **Implement your plan** – and monitor its effects.

Developing a communications plan 12

- ❑ **Get people involved** – encourage appropriate colleagues, members of your team, customers and intermediaries to contribute to your communications strategy and plan.

- ❑ **Marshall the necessary information** – make sure you have relevant, up-to-date information to hand including information on your marketing objectives and alternative means of communication.

- ❑ **Consider your communications options** – decide on the best communications mix of advertising, public relations, sales promotion, direct marketing and direct sales, taking into account their relative benefits and costs.

- ❑ **Define your communications strategy** – define your objectives, message, audience and communications mix and make sure these meet your organisation's objectives and legal requirements.

- ❑ **Present your communications plan** – present your detailed plan including strategy, objectives, audience, marketing message, communications mix, tasks and responsibilities, resources required, time scales, budgets and controls.

- ❑ **Communicate your plan** – when your plan has been approved, make sure all those involved or affected are aware of its implications and their responsibilities.

- ❑ **Implement your plan** – and monitor its effects.

13 Developing a sales strategy

❑ **Get people involved** – encourage appropriate colleagues, members of your team, customers and intermediaries to contribute to developing your sales strategy.

❑ **Marshall the necessary information** – make sure you have relevant, up-to-date information to hand including information on your competitors', or potential competitors', sales strategies, their strengths and weaknesses.

❑ **Consider your sales options** – when considering alternative sales strategies, take into account

- your customers and potential customers – what are their needs and their motivations to buy?
- your products and services – what are their features and benefits and how do these compare with your competitors' products and services?
- your organisation's resources – are you able to reach your customers directly or will you need to work through partners or intermediaries?
- your margins – how much can you afford to spend on selling your products and services?

❑ **Decide on your sales strategy** – select the most cost-effective option which fits with your organisational and marketing objectives.

❑ **Present your sales plan** – include in your plan

- the argued case for your recommended strategy
- how it fits with your organisation's objectives
- a description of products and services, target customers, sales channels and competitors
- a detailed implementation plan identifying sales targets, tasks and responsibilities, resources required, time scales, budgets and controls.

❑ **Communicate your plan** – when your plan has been approved, make sure all those involved or affected are aware of its implications and their responsibilities.

❑ **Implement your plan** – and monitor its effects.

Evaluating marketing activity

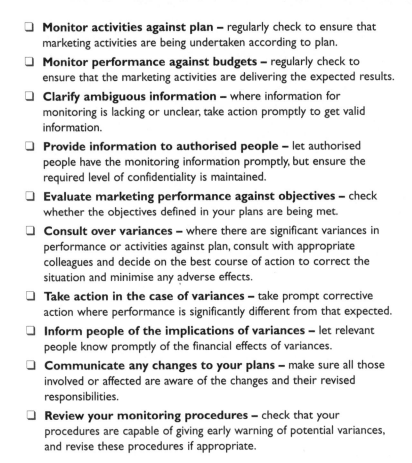

❏ **Monitor activities against plan** – regularly check to ensure that marketing activities are being undertaken according to plan.

❏ **Monitor performance against budgets** – regularly check to ensure that the marketing activities are delivering the expected results.

❏ **Clarify ambiguous information** – where information for monitoring is lacking or unclear, take action promptly to get valid information.

❏ **Provide information to authorised people** – let authorised people have the monitoring information promptly, but ensure the required level of confidentiality is maintained.

❏ **Evaluate marketing performance against objectives** – check whether the objectives defined in your plans are being met.

❏ **Consult over variances** – where there are significant variances in performance or activities against plan, consult with appropriate colleagues and decide on the best course of action to correct the situation and minimise any adverse effects.

❏ **Take action in the case of variances** – take prompt corrective action where performance is significantly different from that expected.

❏ **Inform people of the implications of variances** – let relevant people know promptly of the financial effects of variances.

❏ **Communicate any changes to your plans** – make sure all those involved or affected are aware of the changes and their revised responsibilities.

❏ **Review your monitoring procedures** – check that your procedures are capable of giving early warning of potential variances, and revise these procedures if appropriate.

Managing change

This section is about identifying, implementing and evaluating improvements.

The checklists will help you to

- always be looking for areas where improvements can be made
- assess the benefits against any problems caused by the changes
- prepare plans to make improvements
- consult with all concerned to get them to agree to the changes
- implement your plans for change
- evaluate whether improvements have been achieved.

The process of *Managing change* looks like this.

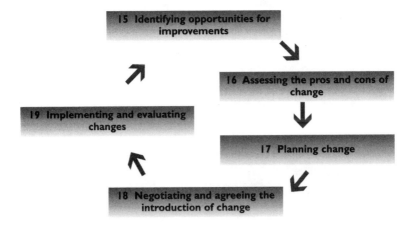

15 Identifying opportunities for improvements

❑ **Keep up to date with developments in your sector** – make sure you get relevant, valid, reliable information from various sources on developments in materials, equipment, technology and processes.

❑ **Consider the importance of these developments to your organisation** – carry out a regular review of developments and analyse their significance to your organisation.

❑ **Pass information on developments to the appropriate people** – if you think it is important, make sure your colleagues, members of your team and senior managers are aware of its significance.

❑ **Identify opportunities for improvements** – use information on developments to identify opportunities for growth, improvements in procedures or improvements in quality.

❑ **Monitor and evaluate your operations continuously** – always look for areas where improvements can be made and take appropriate action.

❑ **Identify any obstacles to change** – take appropriate measures to alleviate any problems which may prevent improvements being made.

❑ **Learn from your experience** – use your experience of previous improvements to help identify new ones.

Assessing the pros and cons of change 16

❑ **Get complete and accurate information** – make sure you have sufficient, reliable information on both current and proposed services, products and processes to allow you to make a reliable assessment.

❑ **Compare the advantages and disadvantages** – use qualitative and quantitative techniques to assess the pros and cons of current and proposed services, products and processes.

❑ **Assess the implications of introducing changes** – changes may affect cash flow, working practices and conditions, health and safety, team morale, supply and distribution networks and customer loyalty; anticipate and assess the likely effect of changes.

❑ **Take into account previous assessments of introducing change** – look at how realistic previous assessments turned out to be and use these to modify your current assessment.

❑ **Present your recommendations to the appropriate people** – make your recommendations to senior managers or specialists in a way which helps them make a decision and in time to allow the decision to be put into effect.

❑ **Amend your recommendations in the light of responses** – make appropriate alterations to your recommendations on the basis of the responses you get from senior managers and specialists.

17 | Planning change

❑ **Provide clear and accurate information** – let those affected know about the proposed change in time for them to prepare effectively.

❑ **Get people involved** – give people the chance to comment on the proposed change and help in the planning.

❑ **Make the case for change** – give a clear and convincing rationale for the change and support this with sound evidence.

❑ **Identify potential obstacles to change** – and find effective ways of avoiding or overcoming these obstacles.

❑ **Develop a detailed plan including**
- the rationale
- the aim and objectives of the change
- how it will be implemented
- who will be involved and their individual roles
- the resources required
- the time scale
- how the plan will be monitored
- how you will know that the change has been successful.

Negotiating and agreeing the introduction of change

18

❑ **Present plans on projected change** – communicate the changes, and the anticipated benefits for your organisation and for individuals, to team members, colleagues, senior managers and others in order to gain their support.

❑ **Conduct negotiations in a spirit of goodwill** – make sure you retain people's support and find mutually acceptable ways of settling any disputes.

❑ **Make compromises where appropriate** – it may be necessary to make compromises to accommodate other priorities, but make sure these compromises are consistent with your organisation's strategy, objectives and practices.

❑ **Reach an agreement in line with your organisation's strategy** – and revise your implementation plans accordingly.

❑ **Keep records of negotiations and agreements** – make sure your records are complete and accurate and that they are available for others to refer to if necessary.

❑ **Where you could not secure the changes you anticipated, tell those affected in a positive manner** – sometimes you are disappointed in not being able to obtain the changes you wanted due to other organisational priorities; explain the reasons for this in a way which maintains people's morale and motivation.

❑ **Encourage all relevant people to understand and participate in the changes** – explain the changes and their effects to people, and gain their support.

19 | Implementing and evaluating changes

❏ **Present details of implementation plans to all concerned –** make sure that you brief everyone involved in the changes, or affected by them, on their role in these changes and the possible impact on their area.

❏ **Encourage people to seek clarification –** check on their understanding of their role and encourage them to ask questions.

❏ **Use resources in the most effective way –** plan carefully so that you meet the new requirements as cost-effectively as possible.

❏ **Maintain quality of work –** ensure that work is maintained to a satisfactory standard during the period of change.

❏ **Monitor the changes –** check to see that the changes have been implemented according to plan and that they result in the improvements anticipated.

❏ **Modify implementation plans and activities in the light of experience –** you may need to modify the way you implement changes to cope with unforeseen problems.

❏ **Evaluate the benefits of the changes –** compare the new way of working with the old; are the benefits as expected?

❏ **Keep records –** keep clear and accurate records of your monitoring and evaluation activities and the results.

❏ **Review the change process –** review the whole process of identifying, assessing, negotiating, agreeing, implementing and evaluating change, note ways of doing it better next time and make appropriate recommendations to senior managers, colleagues and specialists.

→ Project management

This section is about managing projects so that they deliver their agreed outcomes on time, within budget and to the quality required.

The checklists will help you

- arrive at a shared understanding of the goals and scope of the project with your customer
- develop a detailed plan to deliver the project outcomes on time
- estimate the costs involved, develop and agree a realistic budget
- monitor your project, and take action in the event of contingencies or significant deviations from plan
- deliver your project outcomes effectively, provide feedback to those involved and develop opportunities for new work.

As a project manager, you will find that many of the other checklists in the operational management area – managing activities, resources, people and information – will be of use to you during the course of a project.

The process of **Project management** looks like this.

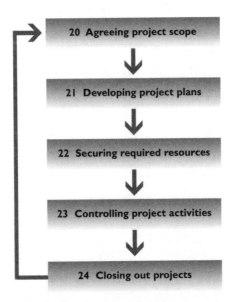

20 Agreeing project scope

21 Developing project plans

22 Securing required resources

23 Controlling project activities

24 Closing out projects

20 Agreeing project scope

❑ **Clarify and agree the project goals with your customer –** whether your customer is internal or external, discuss and agree what they are expecting as a result of the project.

❑ **Identify the constraints on the project –** constraints may be internal to the project (e.g. do you have the necessary resources and technology?), internal to your organisation (e.g. are the financial objectives achievable, does the project fit with your organisation's culture?) or external (e.g. legal, logistic or environmental issues).

❑ **Check that the project is viable –** are the client's goals realistic within the time and resources allowed for the project?

❑ **Agree quality and success criteria with the client –** define the specific quality to which the project must be delivered, and agree how successful completion will be measured.

❑ **Identify and assess risks to the project –** consider
  • the things which may go wrong with the project
  • how likely they are to go wrong
  • what you can do to minimise the risk, or effects, of things going wrong
  • what contingency plans you can make.

❑ **Agree the outline management structure for the project –** how is the work going to be broken down, who will be responsible for what, what reports will be made with what frequency?

❑ **Agree the project contract –** when you and your client have a good shared understanding of the scope of the project, draw up and sign a contract which covers all the key points relating to the contract (your tender document may form part of this contract).

❑ **Review the scope of the project –** periodically check to make sure the project's goal and scope are fundamentally the same; if they have changed substantially, re-negotiate your contract.

Developing project plans 21

- ❑ **Clarify the scope of the project with all concerned** – make sure that everyone involved – customer, managers and those working on the project – understand the scope and goals of the project and their roles within it.
- ❑ **Break the work down into manageable packages** – divide up a major project into mini-projects or work-packages which have defined objectives.
- ❑ **Define the schedule of work-packages** – decide which activities have to be completed before other activities can start (those on the 'critical path') and those which can take place at the same time; make sure all activities can be completed before the end date of the project.
- ❑ **Allocate responsibilities for work-packages** – agree with those managing work-packages (whether they work inside or outside your organisation) exactly what they are responsible for, what you expect delivered, when and for what cost.
- ❑ **Agree working methods** – agree with those responsible the methods they will use to deliver the objectives of the work-packages and the level of autonomy they have for changing working methods.
- ❑ **Agree reporting and monitoring procedures** – agree with the customer and work-package managers
  - how progress will be reported
  - delivery dates for work-packages
  - at what point significant deviations from the plan must be reported.
- ❑ **Define communication procedures** – agree the procedures for regular communication on project progress and for communication in the event of emergencies or contingencies.

22 Securing required resources

- ❏ **Estimate the costs of the project** – look at the resources required for each work-package including
  - labour costs
  - materials costs
  - equipment costs
  - transport costs
  - general costs
  - overhead costs.
- ❏ **Estimate the human resources required** – look at the number and type of personnel required and the different skills they will need.
- ❏ **Estimate the physical resources required** – look at the equipment, materials, premises, energy, services and transport you will need.
- ❏ **Estimate the overhead costs** – what is the proportion of costs of management time, office costs and consumables which you should allocate to this project?
- ❏ **Take account of contingencies** – make an allowance for the things which may go wrong.
- ❏ **Allow for inflation** – if your project is running over a year or more, make sure you allow for any likely increases in costs.
- ❏ **Agree your project budget** – present your overall budget to your customer, agree this budget and how payments and reimbursements will be made.

Controlling project activities

❑ **Agree a baseline plan with all concerned** – make sure everyone involved – the customer, work-package managers and those working on the project – agree to working to, and reporting against, your baseline project plan.

❑ **Authorise any changes** – make sure that you (and your customer, where appropriate) are informed of, and agree to, any significant changes to project activities or working practices.

❑ **Get regular and accurate progress reports** – make sure that you receive progress reports on time, and that these accurately report actual progress against plan.

❑ **Evaluate your progress** – evaluate whether progress is satisfactory and forecast whether the project's objectives will be delivered on time and within budget.

❑ **Discuss your progress** – discuss the progress of your project with your customer, work-package managers and those working on the project, to confirm the actual situation and agree any corrective action required.

❑ **Take corrective action, if required** – if necessary, take appropriate action to get the project back on track to deliver the project's objectives.

❑ **Respond effectively to contingencies** – take appropriate action in the event of emergencies and contingencies; report the situation and your action to your customer as soon as possible.

❑ **Agree changes to the scope of the project** – if the scope of the project, its objectives or the customer's requirements have changed, agree these changes and their implications with the customer.

❑ **Revise the project plan** – make sure all those involved are aware of the changes and how they affect them.

24   Closing out projects

❑ **Deliver the outcomes of the project** – hand over the products and results of the project to your client and other stakeholders involved.

❑ **Confirm the success of the project** – confirm with your customer that the goals and objectives have been achieved to the quality required and against agreed success criteria.

❑ **Evaluate your project** – consider what went well and what went badly; identify and evaluate the reasons for success and failure and the lessons to be learnt.

❑ **Provide feedback to those involved** – provide feedback on performance to work-package managers, those working on the project and also to your customer on how they contributed to the success of the project.

❑ **Celebrate the completion of the project** – take appropriate opportunities to celebrate your shared success and thank and congratulate those involved.

❑ **Publicise your achievements** – look for opportunities to let others know of the success of the project and your, and your organisation's, role in it.

❑ **Develop follow-up opportunities** – make the most of the opportunity to identify and develop potential new projects with your client and other stakeholders.

→ Quality assurance

This section is about developing, implementing and monitoring systems to ensure that you meet your customers' needs on time, every time.

The checklists will help you to

- be clear about your customers' needs and how quality systems can ensure these are met
- involve team members and other colleagues in developing quality assurance systems
- spot unacceptable variations in quality and take action to avoid these becoming problems
- monitor and publicise the benefits of quality assurance systems
- develop a culture of continuous improvement in your organisation.

This section links closely with the sections on **Meeting customer needs** and **Managing change**. It has three checklists.

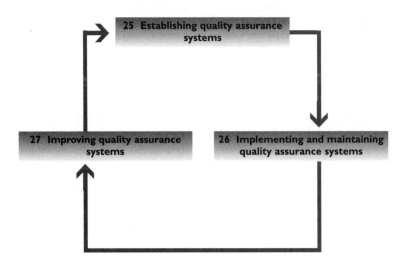

25 Establishing quality assurance systems

27 Improving quality assurance systems

26 Implementing and maintaining quality assurance systems

25 Establishing quality assurance systems

❑ **Establish the rationale for the quality assurance system** – be clear about what you are hoping to achieve and what the benefits will be.

❑ **Be clear about your customers' expectations and requirements** – quality is about fulfilling your customers' expectations on time, every time.

❑ **Get people involved** – ask your team members, colleagues and senior managers to help develop the systems in order to gain their support and commitment.

❑ **Analyse the processes involved in delivering your services and products** – you need to understand each step in the process to decide what systems, procedures and measurements are necessary to ensure your services and products are of acceptable quality.

❑ **Make the best use of resources** – make sure your quality assurance system does not duplicate or add unnecessarily to the workload, but makes best use of existing procedures and activities.

❑ **Develop a detailed implementation plan**, including
  - the rationale
  - the aim and objectives of the quality assurance system
  - how it will be implemented
  - who will be involved and their individual roles
  - the resources required
  - the time scale
  - how the plan will be monitored.

Implementing and maintaining quality assurance systems 26

❏ **Present details of the quality assurance system, or modifications to it, to all those concerned –** make sure that you brief everyone involved or affected by the quality assurance system on their role and the possible impact on their area.

❏ **Encourage people to seek clarification –** check on their understanding of, and commitment to, their role and encourage them to ask questions.

❏ **Monitor the processes and results –** collect and evaluate information and report against agreed performance measures on a regular basis.

❏ **Spot variations in quality promptly –** encourage everyone involved to report actual or potential variations in quality.

❏ **Take corrective action –** where there are unacceptable variations in your services or products, take prompt and effective action in line with your quality assurance procedures.

❏ **Publicise the benefits and results of quality assurance –** enhance employee commitment and customer satisfaction by making sure they are aware of the benefits that the quality assurance system is delivering.

27 | Improving quality assurance systems

❑ **Develop a culture of continuous improvement** – encourage those involved to recommend ways in which processes, conditions and the quality assurance systems themselves can be improved.

❑ **Monitor your quality assurance systems** – check whether they continue to deliver customer satisfaction.

❑ **Make recommendations for improving your quality assurance systems** – make sure your recommendations are clear, well-argued and based on reliable information.

❑ **Implement improvements** – where your recommendations are accepted, implement the improvements without delay.

❑ **Where you could not secure improvements, tell those involved in a positive manner** – sometimes you are disappointed in not being able to obtain the improvements you wanted due to other organisational priorities; explain the reasons for this in a way which maintains people's morale and motivation.

Environmental management

This section is about helping your organisation to minimise any adverse impact it has on the environment and commit to a policy of sustainable development, meeting the needs of the present without compromising the abilities of future generations to meet their own needs.

The checklists will help you to

- identify your organisation's legal, moral, social and economic responsibilities in respect of the environment
- assess the environmental impact of any proposed new development or process
- review your organisation's current environmental performance and the opportunities for improvement
- develop an agreed environmental management policy for your organisation
- develop, implement and monitor an environmental management system for your organisation
- prepare for accidents and emergencies and deal effectively with them should they occur
- regularly audit your organisation's environmental performance against your policy and objectives
- promote good practice in environmental management and your organisation's role in this
- comply with the requirements of the UK's Environmental Protection Act (EPA), the International Standard ISO 14001, the European Union's Environmental Impact Assessment (EIA) Directive and the European Eco-Management and Audit Scheme (EMAS).

The process for *Environmental management* looks like this.

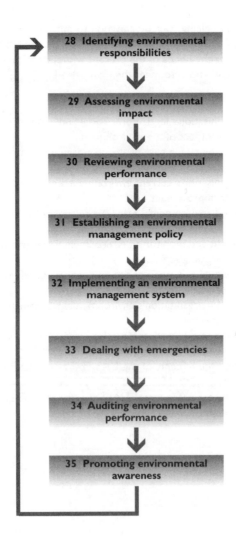

Identifying environmental responsibilities 28

❑ **Monitor your environmental responsibilities** – maintain a system to provide you with up-to-date information about your legal responsibilities, stakeholders' interests and other factors which impact on your organisation.

❑ **Identify your legal responsibilities** – find out what environmental legislation affects your organisation and what you need to do to comply with this legislation.

❑ **Identify your stakeholders' interests** – identify who are your stakeholders (shareholders, customers, employees, local authorities, pressure groups, media etc.) and what their views are regarding your environmental responsibilities.

❑ **Identify relevant organisational values** – be clear what values are held in your organisation which may influence the development of your environmental policy and practices.

❑ **Assess the implications of legislation, stakeholders' interests and values** – consult with colleagues and specialists on how these factors may affect the development of your environmental policy and practices.

❑ **Seek guidance** – where legislation, stakeholders' interests and organisational values are in conflict, seek the advice of colleagues and specialists to resolve the issue.

29 | Assessing environmental impact

❑ **Carry out an environmental impact assessment (EIA)** – when considering setting up a new industrial plant or commercial building, or just implementing a new process, carry out an assessment of the environmental impact this will have.

❑ **Describe the proposed process design** – what is the purpose of the development, its physical attributes, operational characteristics and what emissions, if any, will there be?

❑ **Consider the alternatives** – what are the alternatives in terms of location, product or process design and the way the process will be managed?

❑ **Describe the baseline environment** – what is the current environment like in terms of local population, current site use, natural habitats, air, water and soil quality, landscape and built environment?

❑ **Assess potential environmental impact** – what will be the positive or negative impact of the development in the short, medium and long-terms on the physical, social and economic environments?

❑ **Identify mitigating measures** – decide what technologies, techniques or alternatives you can employ to reduce negative environmental impact and how effective these measures are likely to be.

❑ **Identify contingency measures** – assess the risks involved and decide on the measures you can take in the event of an accident or emergency.

❑ **Evaluate your assessment** – in the light of the information you have gathered, form a judgement on how reliable the various aspects of your assessment are.

❑ **Prepare an environmental impact statement (EIS)** – prepare a report of your findings with a non-technical summary.

❑ **Present your environmental impact statement** – present your report, together with recommendations whether or not to proceed, modifications to the proposed process design or further investigations which need to be carried out before a decision can be made.

Reviewing environmental performance ## 30

❑ **Identify your legal responsibilities** – what laws govern the environmental performance of your organisation and what is your potential exposure to legal liability?

❑ **Identify the key environmental issues affecting your organisation** – where does your organisation have greatest environmental impact, on air, water or land, or on other factors such as noise, odours or landscape?

❑ **Identify your organisation's current environmental performance in terms of**
- how you design, plan and manage your products and services
- the raw materials you use, how these are managed and stored
- the methods of transportation you use
- the waste you create and how this is managed, disposed of and recycled.

❑ **Compare with other similar organisations** – compare your organisation's performance and practices with those of competitors or other similar organisations and identify opportunities for improvement.

❑ **Review your accident and emergency procedures** – what actions have you taken to prevent or mitigate the effects of accidents, emergencies and pollution, and how could these be improved?

❑ **Review the training and information given to staff on environmental issues** – is this adequate and does it ensure their commitment to good environmental practices?

❑ **Review your public relations** – what is your environmental image and relationship like with the local community, customers and the public in general?

❑ **Identify the benefits of improved environmental performance** – these may include new product, service or market opportunities, improved efficiency, better quality, increased staff commitment, improved public relations, reduced risk, lower insurance premiums, cheaper finance and assured compliance with environmental legislation.

❑ **Make recommendations for the development of an environmental policy and the implementation of an environmental management system.**

31 Establishing an environmental management policy

❑ **Consult with key stakeholders –** consult with those who have the greatest legitimate interest in the impact of your organisation on the environment (such as shareholders, employees, local authorities and pressure groups) to ensure their interests are represented.

❑ **Develop your environmental policy –** this may include

- a commitment to sustainable development, meeting the needs of the present without compromising the abilities of future generations to meet their own needs
- a definition of the environmental standards and regulations which must be met, both by your own organisation and by your suppliers, contractors and agents
- the acceptance of responsibility for your products and services throughout their life cycle, from the raw materials used to their disposal after use
- a commitment to the efficient usage of all resources
- a commitment to minimisation of waste, and disposal of waste in a way which is safe and has least impact on the environment
- a commitment to regular environmental audits
- an acceptance of your organisation's liability for environmental damage, accidents or incidents
- a commitment to making your organisation's environmental performance public.

❑ **Check that your policy is practical –** can it be translated into business objectives, activities and procedures which can be monitored and measured?

❑ **Check that your policy is achievable –** make sure that you are able to implement your environmental policy and improve your environmental performance in the areas which are critical to your organisation.

❑ **Consult on your draft environmental policy –** discuss your draft policy with key stakeholders and specialists and revise the policy appropriately in the light of their feedback.

❑ **Publicise your environmental policy –** make sure all those involved and other key stakeholders understand your environmental policy and how it affects them.

Implementing an environmental management system

❏ **Ensure your environmental policy is effectively communicated** – make sure that all those involved understand and are committed to the policy and their responsibilities in relation to it.

❏ **Define management responsibilities** – make sure that the responsibilities for environmental management are clearly defined and that appropriate resources are allocated to implementing the policy.

❏ **Implement education and training programmes** – carry out programmes to ensure that all those involved are competent to carry out their responsibilities.

❏ **Maintain an inventory of environmental effects** – keep a record of all items such as materials, consumption, stock holding, production, releases of substances into the air or water and the disposal of waste, which have an impact on the environment.

❏ **Maintain an inventory of legal requirements** – keep a record of all the environmental legislation which affects your organisation.

❏ **Specify objectives and targets for environmental improvement** – clearly state objectives and targets which are measurable, achievable and consistent with your environmental review and stated policy.

❏ **Plan how objectives are to be achieved** – draw up a detailed action plan, clearly specifying responsibilities, resources and time scales.

❏ **Implement monitoring and control systems** – put in place systems to ensure compliance with your plans.

❏ **Keep records** – keep appropriate records and make these available to authorised people as required.

❏ **Hold regular audits** – carry out regular audits to ensure your environmental management system works and that the targeted improvements are being achieved.

33 Dealing with emergencies

❑ **Identify potential environmental risks and problems** – consult with colleagues and specialists to identify possible risks and problems both in the short and longer-term.

❑ **Evaluate the impact of risks and problems** – develop scenarios of what would happen in different situations if the risks or problems were to materialise.

❑ **Take action to minimise the risks or the impact of problems** – where possible, reduce the risk of accidents and pollution occurring, or reduce the potential environmental impact if they were to happen.

❑ **Develop contingency plans** – develop detailed plans to deal with the possible accidents and emergencies identified.

❑ **Train people to deal with accidents and emergencies** – communicate your contingency plans to all those involved and train them to carry out their responsibilities effectively in the event of an emergency.

❑ **Implement contingency plans** – in the event of an emergency, implement your plans immediately.

❑ **Review contingency plans** – if an emergency does occur, review the effectiveness of your contingency plans and revise them, if necessary.

Auditing environmental performance 34

❑ **Define the scope of the audit** – be clear whether the audit covers all your organisation's activities, or just a single site or product line.

❑ **Recruit the audit team** – recruit a team comprising people with all the technical, industry-specific and auditing competences required.

❑ **Inform people about the audit** – communicate the purpose and scope of the audit to those concerned and the information and co-operation which will be required from them.

❑ **Check for compliance** – check records to ensure that all activities within the audit period comply with the relevant legislation and agreed standards, and report any variances.

❑ **Check that plans and procedures have been followed** – check that plans and procedures as agreed in the environmental management system have been followed, and report any variances.

❑ **Assess actual performance against target** – has your organisation actually achieved the targets it set itself for environmental performance?

❑ **Prepare your audit report** – draft your report including, as appropriate

- executive summary, covering general issues, non-compliance, risks and recommendations
- general environmental factors: air, water, land, noise
- waste management
- energy efficiency
- technology
- health and safety
- fire control and emergency procedures
- special substances
- non-compliance
- prioritised recommendations

❑ **Present your report to senior management** – discuss your report and recommendations with senior managers.

❑ **Develop an action plan** – develop a detailed plan to address current deficiencies and work towards new targets for environmental performance.

35 Promoting environmental awareness

❑ **Publicise your policy, objectives and achievements** – seize opportunities to publicise your organisation's environmental policy, your targets for environmental performance and the results of your environmental audits.

❑ **Develop partnerships** – develop strategic alliances with other organisations such as suppliers, customers, industry organisations, local authorities, local employers or pressure groups to improve environmental standards.

❑ **Support environmentally-friendly activities and causes** – align your organisation with events, activities and campaigns whose objectives are in line with your organisation's values and environmental policy.

CHAPTER 2

Manage people

Management is about meeting customer requirements with and through people.

Managing yourself

This section is about making the most efficient use of your own time, knowledge and skills.

The checklists will help you to

- be clear about your objectives and priorities
- plan your time and allow for contingencies
- delegate work where appropriate
- be decisive
- develop the skills you need to meet your objectives.

This section will help you with all other aspects of management.
Managing yourself covers

36 Managing your time

37 Developing your skills

36 Managing your time

❑ **Be clear about your objectives** – be clear about what you have to achieve, by when and what the priorities are.

❑ **Identify what needs to be done to achieve these objectives** – identify what you, and others, need to do to achieve your objectives and estimate how long each activity will take.

❑ **Plan your time** – plan these activities into your time on an annual, monthly, weekly and daily basis to ensure objectives are achieved on time; include time for evaluation.

❑ **Delegate** – review your activities and, where possible, delegate those activities which could be done equally well by one of your team, with training and guidance where appropriate.

❑ **Handle paper once only** – when dealing with paper, decide immediately to respond, refer, file or destroy.

❑ **Take decisions** – when faced with a choice, either make your choice or decide what further information you need to be able to make an informed choice.

❑ **Control interruptions** – make it clear when you welcome consultation with others, and when you require uninterrupted time to complete an activity.

❑ **Control digressions** – keep your objectives in mind and do not indulge in, or allow others to indulge in, digressions.

❑ **Allow for contingencies** – allow time in your planning for additional activities or for activities to overrun.

❑ **Review your activities** – review your progress towards your objectives on a regular basis and reschedule activities as necessary.

Developing your skills

❑ **Take responsibility for developing yourself** – ensure you develop the skills you need to achieve your objectives.

❑ **Identify your own strengths and weaknesses** – measure your current skills as a manager against appropriate standards, and by getting feedback from your line manager, colleagues and members of your team.

❑ **Set yourself clear development objectives** – make your objectives achievable, realistic and challenging.

❑ **Consider the needs of the organisation** – include objectives to develop as a team member.

❑ **Allow sufficient time and resources** – allocate sufficient time and appropriate resources to achieve your development objectives.

❑ **Get help and support** – ask others to give you coaching and mentoring support and to help you create learning opportunities.

❑ **Regularly review progress and performance** – check your progress against your objectives with your line manager and specialists at regular intervals and revise your plan as appropriate.

❑ **Compare feedback with your own perceptions of your performance** – compare feedback from your line manager, colleagues, team members and others with how well you think you are doing; and improve your future performance as a result.

Personnel planning

This section is about making sure you have the right people to do the jobs.

The checklists will help you to

- be clear about the people you need to meet your organisational objectives
- specify the skills, qualities and attributes you are looking for in team members
- advertise posts to encourage suitable candidates to apply
- assess candidates against specific criteria and select those most appropriate
- make appointments and draw up contracts of employment
- prepare induction programmes
- develop plans to redeploy people
- make redundant those team members who are no longer required.

The process for *Personnel planning* looks like this.

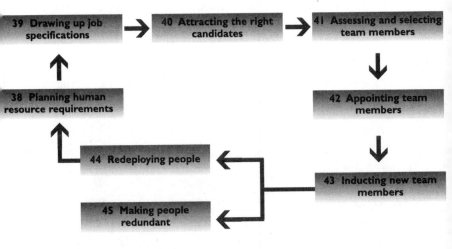

38 | Planning human resource requirements

❑ **Identify the optimum human resources required to achieve objectives** – you will need people to help you achieve the objectives of your organisation, department, team or project; identify the number and type of people needed to provide you with the best support at the most reasonable cost.

❑ **Base your plans on current, valid and reliable information** – check your information is sound and up-to-date.

❑ **Support your plans with appropriate calculations** – your estimates of the human resource required will need to be supported by calculations of the time required to complete tasks and the associated personnel costs, including training and development, and provision for special needs.

❑ **Identify the skills and personal qualities required of the team and individuals** – look for a balance of strengths within the team.

❑ **Be clear about organisational constraints** – specify where financial considerations, organisational policy or legal constraints affect your plans.

❑ **Consult with colleagues and team members** – take into account the views of your colleagues, specialists and members of your team on how best to meet your future human resource requirements.

❑ **Present your plans on time and with the appropriate level of detail** – make sure your plans are accurate, contain sufficient detail for a decision to be made and are presented in time for you to take the necessary action.

Drawing up job specifications

❑ **Be clear about the job role** – clearly state the purpose of the job and how it relates to organisational objectives and the team.

❑ **Specify the job in sufficient detail** – think carefully about the job title, reporting relationships, job purpose, key responsibilities and the terms and conditions of service.

❑ **Specify the type of person required** – be clear about the experience, knowledge, skills, qualifications and personal qualities they will need.

❑ **Consult with colleagues and team members** – take into account the views of your colleagues, specialists and members of your team on the definition of the job and the skills, knowledge and qualities required.

❑ **Check that the specification is clear, concise and complies with legal and organisational requirements** – consult with specialists if you are in doubt.

❑ **Agree the specification with appropriate people** – check and agree the specification with colleagues, specialists and members of your team before taking any action to recruit, transfer or change a person's job.

❑ **Regularly review job specifications** – keep specifications under review to ensure that they still describe the job and meet the organisation's needs.

40 Attracting the right candidates

❏ **Follow your organisation's procedures** – if your organisation has developed procedures or guidelines for recruitment, use these as a guide.

❏ **Consult with colleagues** – ask colleagues for their advice and opinions on how and where you should recruit.

❏ **Publicise the position** – let people know that you are recruiting and the sort of person you are looking for.

❏ **Select appropriate media** – the job description and person specification will help you decide the best way to advertise the job by selecting from a range of appropriate media, including

- local press
- trade or specialist press
- national press
- local radio
- job centres
- staff newsletters
- notice boards
- asking friends and colleagues (word of mouth)
- direct approaches to possible candidates
- using recruitment agencies.

❏ **Draw up your advertisement** – this should include job title, indication of salary, type of contract (permanent, temporary, full or part-time), where the job is based, information on your organisation, brief description of job, type of person required, how to apply, to whom to apply, closing date and address to apply to.

❏ **Comply with legal requirements** – make sure you comply with the laws, particularly those referring to unfair discrimination, which cover recruitment.

❏ **Attract sufficient suitably qualified candidates to allow you to make a good choice.**

Assessing and selecting team members

❑ **Check your organisation's procedures and legal requirements** – make sure that your process for assessing and selecting team members complies with your organisation's procedures and the law.

❑ **Obtain, or draw up, criteria against which to judge candidates** – have clear, measurable criteria.

❑ **Seek advice if you are not sure about any of the selection criteria** – consult with specialists if you are in doubt.

❑ **Get sufficient information from candidates to be able to make a decision** – use a variety of appropriate assessment techniques, cv's, application forms, interviews, tests, references etc., to ensure you get all relevant information.

❑ **Judge the information obtained against specified selection criteria** – you should be able to defend your decision to accept or reject a candidate by how well the candidates meet the selection criteria; do not let irrelevant factors affect your decision.

❑ **Be fair and consistent** – correct any deviations from agreed procedures before you make your selection.

❑ **Maintain confidentiality** – tell only authorised people of your selection recommendations.

❑ **Keep clear, accurate and complete records** – you may need to refer back to them.

❑ **Keep candidates informed** – tell candidates promptly and accurately of decisions following each stage of the selection process and give them appropriate feedback on how well they did.

❑ **Check that your choice is justifiable** – make sure you have selected the most suitable candidate from the evidence obtained and the process used; if in doubt, consult colleagues or specialists.

❑ **Review the process and make appropriate recommendations for improvement** – consider every aspect of the process and make any recommendations for improving it, so that you and your colleagues can do better next time.

47 | **Appointing team members**

❑ **Confirm all details** – check that you have all necessary information and that your selection process complies with your organisation's procedures and with the law.

❑ **Agree appointment with relevant people** – check that those involved in the selection process, personnel specialists and senior management agree with the appointment.

❑ **Make a clear job offer** – even if you offer the job face-to-face or by telephone, follow up with a letter, including job title, salary, holiday and pension entitlement, other benefits, terms and conditions, start date and place and who they should report to; make it clear if the offer is subject to satisfactory references or medical report.

❑ **Take up references** – write or telephone to referees; ask specific questions to confirm the information you have about the new member of your team and to allay any doubts you may have.

❑ **Confirm the appointment** – or withdraw the offer if references or the medical report is unsatisfactory.

❑ **Provide a written contract of employment** – agree and sign a contract of employment within three months of the date of appointment.

❑ **Prepare the work space** – make sure the new team member has a suitable work space with all the equipment necessary to be productive.

❑ **Prepare an induction programme** – prepare a programme to introduce the new team member to colleagues in your organisation and gain the essential knowledge and skills to be productive.

❑ **Inform colleagues** – let people know about the arrival of the new team member, their role and reporting arrangements; ask colleagues to make the new arrival welcome.

Inducting new team members

❑ **Welcome the new team member** – make yourself available to welcome people, on arrival if possible.

❑ **Provide an induction programme for each new team member** – this may include

- information about the organisation
- introductions to colleagues
- introductions to the work environment
- instructions about the job
- briefings on work procedures
- meetings with specialists
- background reading to gain useful knowledge about the job
- training in skills and techniques specific to your organisation
- training in skills and knowledge identified as lacking through the selection process
- individual requirements.

❑ **Assign a mentor or adviser** – ask an experienced team member to make themselves available to provide advice and information to the new team member and generally make them feel welcome.

❑ **Encourage people to take responsibility for their own induction programmes** – make it their responsibility to complete the programme, make appointments to see people and amend the programme as appropriate.

❑ **Monitor the induction programme** – book times in your diary to check that all is going well.

❑ **Evaluate the induction programme** – check that it has been completed successfully and agree any further development required.

❑ **Get feedback** – ask the new team member for their initial impressions of the organisation, their colleagues and their induction programme; make recommendations for improvement as appropriate.

44 Redeploying people

❑ **Keep people informed about current procedures** – ensure that members of your team are aware of your organisation's policy and any redeployment procedures, including appeals procedure.

❑ **Consult with team members** – consult with both individual team members and their representatives over any possible redeployment. Consultation will improve co-operation and may result in alternative, more cost-effective approaches being adopted.

❑ **Agree clear and fair selection criteria** – agree criteria for selecting those to be redeployed which are unambiguous, can be clearly applied, are fair and comply with legal and organisational requirements.

❑ **Apply selection criteria fairly and consistently** – consult with specialists if you are in doubt.

❑ **Make a clear redeployment offer** – although you will probably make the offer face-to-face, support this with a letter specifying the new job, its location, who they will report to, any changes in salary, benefits or other terms and conditions and any relocation allowances. Make it clear what the alternatives are if the offer is not accepted.

❑ **Allow a reasonable time to consider the offer** – take into account the individual's personal circumstances as well as the urgency for your organisation.

❑ **Provide help and support** – provide the necessary help and support to enable those redeployed quickly to become productive in their new roles and situations.

❑ **Seek advice** – seek advice from colleagues and specialists on all aspects of redeployment in order to ensure you comply with legal and organisational requirements.

❑ **Keep people informed** – tell team members and colleagues about the redeployment and the reason, without breaching confidentiality.

❑ **Recommend any changes to policy or procedures** – tell the appropriate people of ways in which your organisation's policy or procedures could be improved.

Making people redundant

- ❏ **Keep people informed about current procedures** – ensure that team members are aware of your organisation's policy and any redundancy procedures, including appeals procedure.
- ❏ **Avoid redundancies where possible** – accurate personnel planning will minimise the need for redundancies, but where these are inevitable explore alternatives such as early retirement or part-time working.
- ❏ **Consult with people** – consult with both individual team members and their representatives over the redundancy plan. Consultation will improve co-operation and may result in alternative, more acceptable approaches being adopted.
- ❏ **Agree clear and fair selection criteria** – agree selection criteria which are unambiguous, can be clearly applied, are fair and comply with legal and organisational requirements.
- ❏ **Apply selection criteria fairly and consistently** – consult with specialists if you are in doubt.
- ❏ **Prepare to break the news** – rehearse what you will say to people who will be made redundant, including responses to likely questions.
- ❏ **Break the news quickly and compassionately** – tell the people concerned quickly, clearly, confidentially and compassionately that they will be made redundant and what help is available to them.
- ❏ **Offer alternative work** – where there are suitable jobs available, offer these alternatives with details of terms and conditions.
- ❏ **Offer counselling** – offer the people concerned appropriate counselling, resources, training and time off work to help them find another job and cope with the personal and practical implications of redundancy.
- ❏ **Seek advice** – seek advice from colleagues and specialists, on all aspects of making people redundant in order to ensure you comply with legal and organisational requirements.
- ❏ **Keep people informed** – tell team members and colleagues about the redundancies and the reasons, without breaching confidentiality.
- ❏ **Recommend any changes to policy or procedures** – tell the appropriate people of ways in which your organisation's policy or procedures could be improved.

Developing teams and individuals

This section is about making sure your team has the skills to do their jobs.

The checklists will help you to

■ develop a balanced team with all the skills needed
■ help individuals identify and develop the skills they need
■ coach individuals to develop new skills
■ be an adviser or mentor to individuals to help them develop
■ assess team members against development objectives
■ evaluate and improve the training and development processes.

The process for *Developing teams and individuals* looks like this.

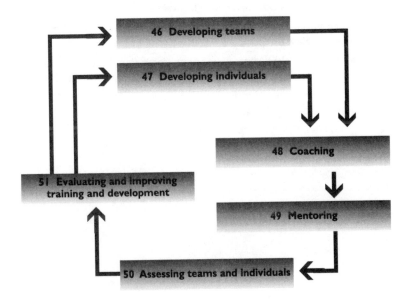

46 Developing teams

❑ **Involve all team members in evaluating the team's development needs** – get them involved in identifying their own strengths and weaknesses.

❑ **Assess the team's strengths and weaknesses** – looking at each individual and at the team as a whole, assess and acknowledge the team's strengths and weaknesses to carry out current and future work.

❑ **Consult with all team members on how to meet development needs** – gain the team's commitment by involving them in planning how to meet development needs.

❑ **Prioritise** – where the resources available are not sufficient to cover all development needs, decide which needs must be addressed in order to meet your organisation's objectives.

❑ **Be clear about the objectives of development plans** – your objectives should be clear, relevant and realistic for individuals and the team as a whole.

❑ **Optimise the use of resources** – when planning development activities, use available resources effectively.

❑ **Provide equal opportunity** – provide equal access to development activities to all team members.

❑ **Lead by example** – show your commitment to individual and team development through your personal support and involvement.

❑ **Minimise unproductive friction** – be clear about individuals' responsibilities in the team to minimise any risk of bad feeling.

❑ **Regularly review your plans** – discuss and agree improvements to development plans with team members, other colleagues and specialists at appropriate intervals.

Developing individuals

❑ **Involve individuals in identifying their own development needs** – get them to identify their own strengths and weaknesses.

❑ **Discuss development needs and plans with individuals** – gain their commitment by involving individuals in planning how to meet their development needs.

❑ **Be clear about the objectives of development plans** – objectives should be clear, relevant and realistic for the individual.

❑ **Balance business needs with individual aspirations** – plans should help individuals to develop the skills they need to do their current job and meet future job requirements and career aspirations.

❑ **Optimise the use of resources** – when planning development activities, use available resources effectively.

❑ **Provide equal opportunity** – provide equal access to development activities to all individuals.

❑ **Monitor individual development** – provide mentoring or coaching support where necessary.

❑ **Regularly review the plans** – regularly discuss and agree improvements to development plans with individuals, other colleagues and specialists.

48 Coaching

- ❑ **Identify the individual's current level of skill** – use appropriate methods to assess the current skills of the person you are coaching.
- ❑ **Agree learning objectives** – discuss and agree with the individual the level of skill to be acquired.
- ❑ **Analyse the components of skills** – make sure you understand the different components of the skills and the sequence in which they need to be learnt.
- ❑ **Agree the steps to be taken** – decide with the individual what steps need to be taken to achieve the desired objectives.
- ❑ **Take account of the individual** – design your coaching to match the individual's learning preferences, and deliver the coaching in a manner and at a pace appropriate to the learner.
- ❑ **Identify inhibiting factors** – clearly identify and discuss with learners any factors which are inhibiting their learning.
- ❑ **Check on the individual's progress** – check regularly on progress and modify coaching as appropriate.
- ❑ **Give feedback** – provide timely feedback to the individual on the process of learning and on their progress towards learning objectives in a positive and encouraging manner.
- ❑ **Receive feedback** – ask learners how they feel about the process of learning and their speed of progress, and modify coaching as appropriate.

Mentoring 49

❑ **Identify individuals' learning objectives** – discuss and identify the learning objectives to be achieved with individuals, their line managers and others involved.

❑ **Agree the support individuals require** – specify and agree the roles, responsibilities and resources needed to help individuals achieve their learning objectives.

❑ **Identify and overcome any difficulties in obtaining this support** – identify likely difficulties in obtaining the necessary people and resources and agree ways of overcoming these difficulties.

❑ **Develop effective working relationships** – both with the individuals and with others who can provide support.

❑ **Provide guidance** – provide accurate, timely and appropriate advice and guidance on learning methods and opportunities, and on other sources of information and advice.

❑ **Encourage independent decision-making** – provide guidance in a way which encourages individuals to take responsibility for their own development and enables them to make informed decisions.

❑ **Facilitate learning and assessment opportunities** – identify and facilitate opportunities for individuals to develop, practise, apply and assess new skills, knowledge and experience in a structured way.

❑ **Provide on-going support** – within the agreed role, provide individuals with support for their learning, development and assessment, as required.

❑ **Give feedback** – provide timely feedback to individuals on their progress towards learning objectives in a positive and encouraging manner.

❑ **Review the mentoring process** – at appropriate intervals, discuss the mentoring process and your relationship with those being provided with guidance, and modify as appropriate.

50   Assessing teams and individuals

❏ **Be clear about the purpose of the assessment** – is it to identify further development needs, appraise performance or provide recognition of knowledge, skills and competence at work?

❏ **Get people involved** – give team members the opportunity to contribute to their own and their team's assessments.

❏ **Provide equal opportunity** – provide equal access to assessment to all team members.

❏ **Develop objective criteria** – develop and agree clear criteria which are consistent with the development objectives and with your organisation's policies.

❏ **Use appropriate assessment methods** – these may include testing of knowledge and skills, observation of performance at work, contributions from other team members and appraisal discussions.

❏ **Make assessment decisions against the criteria** – base your decisions on matching the information you obtain from the assessment processes against the agreed criteria.

❏ **Give feedback** – provide teams and individuals with feedback on their assessments in a positive and encouraging manner.

❏ **Keep clear, accurate and complete records of assessments** – you may wish to refer back to them.

❏ **Maintain confidentiality** – tell only authorised people of the results of assessments.

Evaluating and improving training and development | 51

- ❑ **Identify the training and development objectives** – be clear what the objectives are and how to measure whether they have been achieved.

- ❑ **Debrief the learners** – discuss with individuals and teams involved in training and development how useful it was, how satisfied they were with its delivery and how well it will apply to their work.

- ❑ **Identify the impact of the training and development on your business** – what are the benefits compared with the costs? What would have been the negative impact if you had not trained and developed your people?

- ❑ **Check whether objectives have been achieved** – apply the agreed measures to see to what extent objectives have been achieved.

- ❑ **Find suitable alternatives where training and development did not meet the needs** – discuss and agree with the individuals and teams concerned alternative training and development which may be more appropriate.

- ❑ **Modify team and individual training and development plans** – where plans were unrealistic, discuss and agree modified plans with the teams and individuals concerned.

- ❑ **Pass on your experience** – discuss the strengths and weaknesses of the training and development processes used with specialists, your line manager and colleagues so they can gain from your experience.

- ❑ **Benefit from your experience** – use your experience of training and development processes to help you identify more appropriate and cost-effective training and development in the future.

Managing teams and individuals

This section is about making sure your team get the job done.

The checklists will help you to

■ plan the work to meet your objectives
■ allocate work amongst the team
■ set clear objectives for each member of the team
■ evaluate performance and provide feedback to teams and individuals.

The process for **Managing teams and individuals** looks like this.

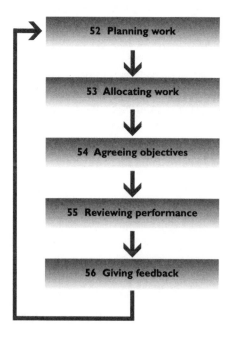

52 Planning work

↓

53 Allocating work

↓

54 Agreeing objectives

↓

55 Reviewing performance

↓

56 Giving feedback

52 Planning work

❏ **Plan work in order to meet organisational objectives –** make sure your plans are consistent with team and organisational objectives.

❏ **Assess the degree of direction required by each team member –** inexperienced or less confident people may need far more direction and help in planning their work than more experienced and self-assured colleagues.

❏ **Encourage individuals to contribute to planning work activities and methods –** the team members who will be carrying out the work are likely to have sound ideas as to the most efficient ways of doing it.

❏ **Include the team's suggestions on working methods, resources and time required –** this will help to ensure their commitment to the work.

❏ **Select work methods and activities which meet both operational and developmental objectives –** choose work methods and activities which balance management priorities, organisational objectives, legal requirements and opportunities for individual development.

❏ **Select cost-effective work methods –** choose work methods which make the best use of available materials, capital and people.

❏ **Seek advice where legal requirements and organisational and developmental objectives conflict –** consult with your line manager, specialists or external advisers.

Allocating work 53

- ❏ **Allocate work according to availability of resources and skills of team members** – optimise the resources and the skills of the team members available to meet organisational objectives.
- ❏ **Clearly define team and individual responsibilities and limits of authority** – make sure team members understand their own responsibilities and limits of authority, and those with whom they work closely, in order to avoid possible conflict, duplication or omission of important responsibilities.
- ❏ **Provide learning and developmental opportunities for team members within the work allocated** – take opportunities to develop new skills which team members will need in the future.
- ❏ **Brief team members on their work in a manner and at a level and pace which is appropriate** – inexperienced or less confident people may need a more detailed briefing on their responsibilities and work than their more experienced and self-assured colleagues.
- ❏ **Encourage people to seek clarification** – check on their understanding and give them opportunities to ask questions.
- ❏ **Provide access to people who can help them meet their objectives** – team members may need access to colleagues, managers, specialists and external advisers to help them meet their work and developmental objectives.
- ❏ **Provide the right level of supervision** – some team members will require much closer supervision than others.
- ❏ **Ensure that work allocations are realistic** – carefully calculate the time, cost and criticality of the work to ensure appropriate resources have been allocated.
- ❏ **Reallocate work where appropriate** – if the way work was allocated proves to be unrealistic, or organisational demands change, reallocate work whilst minimising any detrimental impact on time or cost.
- ❏ **Benefit from your experience** – evaluate how well you have allocated work in order to improve your performance in the future.

54 Agreeing objectives

❑ **Involve team members in setting objectives** – ask them to be proactive in identifying what their objectives should be.

❑ **Set clear objectives** – agree SMART objectives with your team members which are

- Specific — be precise about what must be achieved
- Measurable — how will you know if it has been achieved?
- Achievable and Agreed — by you, the individual and the team
- Realistic — objectives have to be achievable
- Time-bound — to be completed by a specified time.

❑ **Explain objectives clearly** – when explaining objectives, think about the person you are talking to, and make sure you communicate with them in a manner and at a pace which is appropriate.

❑ **Encourage people to seek clarification** – check on their understanding and give them opportunities to ask questions.

❑ **Decide on work methods** – discuss and agree with team members how they are going to achieve objectives.

❑ **Identify the skills and knowledge required** – do your team members have these skills and knowledge? If not, what plans are in place to make sure they acquire them?

❑ **Agree the measures of performance** – agree how you will know if the objective has been achieved satisfactorily. What evidence will you want to see?

❑ **Update objectives regularly** – review objectives as often as appropriate in the light of changes to individual and team workloads and organisational priorities.

❑ **Agree a date to review performance** – as part of the objective-setting process, agree the date when you will review with your team members whether their objectives have been achieved.

Reviewing performance 55

❑ **Be clear about the purpose of the review** – the purpose could be

- to check that objectives have been achieved
- to check the quality of work and that customer requirements have been met
- to appraise the performance of teams or individuals
- to recognise competent performance and achievement
- to decide on bonuses or other financial rewards.

❑ **Get people involved** – give individuals the opportunity to evaluate their own and their team's performance.

❑ **Provide equal opportunity** – provide equal access to performance review to all team members.

❑ **Evaluate performance** – assess actual performance against the measures agreed when setting objectives, taking into account any changes in circumstances.

❑ **Make appraisal decisions** – decide how well teams and individuals have performed. Have they met their objectives? Were there mitigating circumstances? What additional contributions have they made to the success of your organisation?

❑ **Share your appraisal decisions with teams and individuals** – allow them to say how far they agree with your decision.

❑ **Keep clear and accurate records of performance reviews** – you may need to refer back to them.

❑ **Maintain confidentiality** – tell only authorised people of the results of performance reviews.

56 Giving feedback

❑ **Seek opportunities to provide feedback to teams and individuals on their performance** – feedback helps people to understand if they are doing a good job or if there are areas in which they can improve. Feedback can be given formally or informally, orally or in writing.

❑ **Choose an appropriate time and place to give the feedback** – feedback is more useful and relevant if provided quickly. Sometimes it is appropriate to give feedback publicly, but often a quiet word with a member of your team is what is required.

❑ **Recognise good performance and achievement** – take opportunities to congratulate people on their successes.

❑ **Provide constructive suggestions and encouragement for improving future performance** – when people are not performing well, tell them, and advise them how they can improve.

❑ **Encourage people to contribute to their own assessment** – ask open-ended questions about how they view their performance and invite them to be specific.

❑ **Provide feedback in sufficient detail and in a manner and at a level and pace which is appropriate to the people concerned** – some team members may readily understand your feedback on their performance; with others it may be necessary to be very specific about their performance and any improvements required.

❑ **Encourage people to seek clarification** – check their understanding and give them the opportunity to ask questions.

❑ **Encourage people to make suggestions on how systems and procedures could be improved** – their performance may be greatly enhanced by changes to procedures and working practices.

❑ **Record details of any action agreed** – make a note of actions agreed to maintain or improve their performance or to change procedures, and inform the appropriate people.

❑ **Review performance** – check back at an appropriate point to see whether performance has improved or been maintained.

Working relationships

This section is about building effective working relationships with all those you work with.

The checklists will help you to

- take time to build effective working relationships
- consult with colleagues and keep them informed
- be honest and open with people
- provide support and keep your promises
- take steps to minimise any possible conflicts.

This section covers

57 Building a good reporting relationship

❑ **Keep those to whom you report informed** – provide an appropriate level of detail about activities, progress, results and achievements.

❑ **Provide information about emerging threats and opportunities** – let those to whom you report know about possible threats and opportunities clearly, accurately and with the appropriate level of urgency.

❑ **Seek information and advice** – ask those to whom you report for information and advice on policy and ways of working whenever appropriate.

❑ **Present clear proposals for action** – present proposals at the appropriate time and with the right level of detail. The greater the degree of change, expenditure and risk involved in your proposal, the greater will be the detail required.

❑ **Identify the reasons why a proposal has been rejected** – try to find out clearly what the reasons are and, if appropriate, put forward alternative proposals.

❑ **Make efforts to maintain a good relationship with those to whom you report** – even if you do have disagreements, try to prevent these damaging your relationship.

❑ **Meet your objectives** – always try to fulfil the objectives you have agreed in full; where circumstances prevent you from meeting objectives, inform those to whom you report at the earliest possible time.

❑ **Support those to whom you report** – give them your backing, especially in situations which involve people outside your team.

❑ **Be open and direct** – discuss any concerns about the relationship directly and, if possible, face-to-face.

Building relationships with your team | 58

- ❏ **Take time to build honest and constructive relationships –** get to know your team and allow them to get to know you.
- ❏ **Keep your team informed –** provide them with relevant information on organisational policy and strategy, progress, emerging threats and opportunities.
- ❏ **Consult about proposed activities –** give team members the opportunity to state their views so they can be taken into account.
- ❏ **Encourage your team to offer their ideas and views –** use open questions to get their contributions.
- ❏ **Give people recognition for their ideas and views –** thank them and show them that you value their ideas.
- ❏ **When suggestions are not taken up, explain the reasons clearly –** where it is not possible to take up a good idea, acknowledge the value of the idea and explain why it is not possible to adopt it.
- ❏ **Encourage people to seek clarification –** check their understanding and give them the opportunity to ask questions.
- ❏ **Keep your promises –** when you make promises and undertakings to your team, make sure they are realistic and that you honour them.
- ❏ **Support your team –** give them your backing especially in situations which involve people outside your team.
- ❏ **Be open and direct –** discuss concerns about the quality of work directly with the relevant member of your team.

59 Building relationships with colleagues

❏ **Take time to build honest and constructive relationships with colleagues** – get to know your colleagues and allow them to get to know you.

❏ **Encourage open, honest and friendly behaviour** – ask open questions to get their opinions.

❏ **Share information and opinions with colleagues** – stop and think who could benefit from any information or idea you have.

❏ **Offer help and advice with sensitivity** – you can often help a colleague or provide advice on a difficult problem.

❏ **Deal courteously with colleagues when you have differences of opinion** – you will not always agree with colleagues; discuss these different views respectfully and try to understand them.

❏ **Resolve conflicts amicably** – always maintain mutual respect.

❏ **Keep your promises** – when you make promises to colleagues, make sure they are realistic and that you honour your commitments.

Minimising conflict

❏ **Explain the standards of work and behaviour you expect –** some people will readily appreciate the standards you and your organisation require; others may require a fuller and more detailed explanation.

❏ **Clearly allocate work and responsibilities –** you can greatly reduce the potential for conflict by making sure your team are clear about the responsibilities of each member.

❏ **Encourage people to discuss problems which affect their work –** make it clear that you are available to help resolve these problems.

❏ **Identify potential or actual conflicts quickly –** when conflicts appear, or are likely, involve the relevant individuals in identifying the nature and cause of the conflict early on.

❏ **Take prompt action to resolve conflicts –** do not let the conflict fester, but take decisive action to deal with it.

❏ **Ensure solutions satisfy legal and organisational requirements** – check that you are not infringing any legislation or procedures and that your solution helps meet your organisation's objectives.

❏ **Keep accurate and complete records of the conflict –** particularly where the conflict is serious, keep notes of what happened and what was agreed, in case there is any comeback.

❏ **Monitor the situation –** keep an eye on the situation to ensure that the conflict does not re-emerge.

❏ **Learn from your experience –** use the experience to help you and your team avoid conflicts or resolve them speedily in the future.

Managing problems with your team

This section is about ensuring the best outcome when you have problems with your team.

The checklists will help you to

■ counsel people when personal matters are affecting their work
■ action grievance and disciplinary procedures
■ dismiss people, where this is the most appropriate option.

This section covers

61 Counselling

62 Implementing grievance and disciplinary procedures

63 Dismissing people

61 Counselling

- ❑ **Identify the need for counselling quickly** – be alert to the need to counsel team members; changes in mood, a fall-off in performance, stress symptoms, or a word from a colleague may indicate the need to counsel individuals.

- ❑ **Choose an appropriate time and place** – counselling on personal matters affecting an individual's work needs to take place in a private place and at a time which allows for full discussion without interruptions.

- ❑ **Follow your organisation's guidelines or personnel policies** – if your organisation has specified personnel policies, check to make sure you follow these.

- ❑ **Encourage the individual to discuss the situation fully** – help the individual to understand the situation and all the relevant factors.

- ❑ **Encourage the individual to take responsibility for their own decisions and actions** – remember you are helping someone to solve a problem, you are not solving it for them.

- ❑ **Recommend an appropriate counselling service where appropriate** – when you do not have the skills or knowledge to help the individual, recommend they see a specialist in your organisation or an external professional service.

- ❑ **Monitor the situation** – keep an eye on the situation and offer further counselling sessions if these are necessary.

- ❑ **Maintain confidentiality** – keep all documents confidential and only discuss the situation with authorised people.

Implementing grievance and disciplinary procedures

❏ **Keep your team informed about current procedures** – make sure they have up-to-date copies of your organisation's grievance and disciplinary procedures and remind them of these from time to time.

❏ **Action grievance and disciplinary procedures with minimum delay** – act promptly to prevent the situation getting out of hand and causing damage to your organisation or the people concerned.

❏ **Act in accordance with legal and organisational requirements** – check, with a specialist if necessary, both the legal situation and your organisation's procedures.

❏ **Ask for advice** – where appropriate, ask a specialist, your line manager or colleagues for confidential advice on how to deal effectively with these difficult situations, especially where legal and organisational requirements conflict.

❏ **Involve a third party – where appropriate, ask a third party – specialist, senior manager or colleague** – to become involved to ensure you implement the procedures fairly and impartially.

❏ **Be, and be seen to be, impartial** – get all the facts of the case before you and make decisions which are objective and can be shown to be free of personal bias.

❏ **Keep accurate and complete records** – make detailed notes of the whole proceedings and, where appropriate, copy these to the people concerned and to specialists.

❏ **Monitor the situation** – keep an eye on the situation to ensure that the problems which triggered the implementation of grievance or disciplinary procedures do not re-emerge.

❏ **Learn from your experience** – use the experience to help you, and members of your team, to avoid the problems or to resolve them quickly in the future.

❏ **Recommend any improvements to the procedures** – tell the appropriate people of any ways in which the procedures could be improved.

63 Dismissing people

❏ **Avoid the need to dismiss people wherever possible** – good recruitment and selection, training, development and counselling techniques will minimise the need for dismissals.

❏ **Follow disciplinary procedures** – make sure you follow your organisation's disciplinary procedures in detail.

❏ **Seek advice** – seek advice from colleagues and specialists, inside or outside your organisation, on all aspects of dismissals in order to ensure you comply with legal and organisational requirements.

❏ **Involve a third party** – where appropriate, ask a specialist, senior manager or colleague to become involved to ensure you follow procedures fairly and impartially.

❏ **Get the facts** – make sure you get all information relevant to the dismissal. If necessary, suspend the individual on full pay until you have all the facts available.

❏ **Prepare to break the news** – rehearse what you will say to the person being dismissed, including responses to likely questions, and enlist the support of colleagues or specialists as appropriate.

❏ **Give clear, fair grounds for dismissal** – check that your reasons for dismissing the team member are clear and fair, and give these both orally and in writing.

❏ **Summarily dismiss individuals in the case of gross misconduct** – dismiss people without notice, or pay in lieu of notice, in the event of gross misconduct. When in doubt, suspend on full pay until you can consult specialists or gather all the facts.

❏ **Minimise disruption** – it is often wise to ensure that a dismissed employee leaves the workplace immediately, to avoid affecting other colleagues.

❏ **Keep people informed** – tell team members and colleagues about the dismissal and the reasons, without breaching confidentiality.

❏ **Review the procedures and reasons for dismissal** – tell the appropriate people of any ways in which the procedures could be improved or future dismissals avoided.

Equal opportunities

This section is about providing equal working opportunities, encouraging diversity and discouraging unfair discrimination.

The checklists will help you to

■ develop, implement and evaluate your equal opportunities policy and action plan
■ encourage people to use a range of appropriate working styles
■ promote fair working practices.

The process of managing *Equal opportunities* looks like this.

64 Promoting equal opportunities

↓

65 Encouraging diversity and fair working practices

Promoting equal opportunities

❏ **Contribute to the development of your organisation's equal opportunities policy** – offer your views and recommendations on how the policy should be developed.

❏ **Involve team members, colleagues and customers** – encourage them to help develop your equal opportunities action plan, identify areas where opportunities are unfairly restricted and gain their commitment to the plan.

❏ **Agree measures** – specify the criteria by which you can assess progress in your action plan.

❏ **Collect and analyse information** – find out whether some groups of potential customers are excluded from obtaining your services or products; check whether certain employees, or potential employees, are denied access to development, employment or promotion opportunities.

❏ **Identify the strengths of all employees** – especially those from under-represented groups, and identify how these strengths can contribute to your organisation's objectives.

❏ **Identify special needs** – identify any special needs of customers, potential customers, employees or potential employees.

❏ **Publish your action plan** – including actions to meet special needs and address any imbalances, as well as taking positive action to support under-represented groups.

❏ **Communicate your action plan to people** – make sure team members are aware of their responsibilities and duties within the equal opportunities policy and the action plan.

❏ **Provide training and development opportunities** – provide appropriate training and development to help team members fulfil their duties in the action plan.

❏ **Implement your action plan and evaluate your performance** – use agreed measures to monitor your progress against the action plan and modify the plan as appropriate.

Encouraging diversity and fair working practices   65

☐ **Communicate your equal opportunities policy to employees –** make sure everyone is aware of the standards of behaviour expected of them and the consequences of unacceptable behaviour.

☐ **Encourage a diversity of working styles –** encourage members of your team to develop a repertoire of appropriate working styles.

☐ **Support natural working styles and behaviour –** encourage members of your team to use their natural and preferred working style and behaviour as long as they are consistent with the achievement of your organisational objectives.

☐ **Discourage stereotyping –** discourage people from imposing stereotypes and styles of working which are inconsistent with individuals' backgrounds.

☐ **Discourage rigid approaches –** where particular styles of working are inhibited without good work-related reasons, provide feedback and suggestions to encourage more diverse approaches.

☐ **Give feedback and suggestions sensitively –** where the style of working is inhibiting achievement of objectives, give feedback and suggestions to individuals in ways which are sensitive to their racial, social, gender or physical circumstances.

☐ **Challenge discriminatory behaviour –** clearly explain the problems this behaviour may cause and the sanctions which will be applied if it continues.

☐ **Implement disciplinary procedures –** take prompt action where unfair discriminatory behaviour persists.

☐ **Seek guidance and support –** where you are unsure of the effect on another person of your own behaviour or that of a team member or colleague, seek guidance and support from specialists, inside or outside your organisation.

CHAPTER 3

Manage resources

Manage resources is about obtaining and using physical resources – money, materials, supplies, equipment, premises and energy – in the most efficient way.

Managing physical resources

This section is about making sure you and your team use physical resources, such as equipment, materials, services, energy and premises, efficiently to achieve your team's objectives.

The checklists will help you to

- identify and secure the resources you need for your work
- monitor the use of resources
- make the most effective use of physical resources.

The process for **Managing physical resources** looks like this.

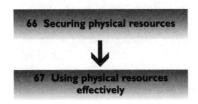

66   Securing physical resources

❑ **Get people involved** – encourage your team members to identify what resources are needed.

❑ **Use your experience** – when drawing up resourcing plans, take account of the way resources have been used in the past.

❑ **Consider trends and developments** – look at what is happening at the moment and at factors which are likely to affect resource usage in the future.

❑ **Develop consistent resourcing plans** – check that your plans are in line with your organisation's objectives and policies and with legal requirements.

❑ **State the resources you need** – base your estimates on past experience, current trends and developments and factors likely to affect resource usage in the future.

❑ **Show the benefits** – state clearly what are the potential benefits arising from the use of the planned resources.

❑ **State your assumptions** – make it clear what assumptions you have made and why.

❑ **Present your plans enthusiastically** – demonstrate the commitment and drive of those who will be using the resources.

❑ **Negotiate where necessary** – be prepared to adapt your plans, but ensure you have sufficient resources to support all the activities within your control.

❑ **Amend your plans** – where you cannot secure all the resources you need, amend your plans appropriately and agree these changes with all concerned.

Using physical resources effectively 67

- ❑ **Share responsibility** – encourage your team members to take individual and collective responsibility for using resources efficiently.
- ❑ **Monitor the quality of resources continuously** – check the quality of your resources to ensure consistent product or service delivery.
- ❑ **Monitor the use of resources against your plan** – make sure your monitoring methods are reliable and comply with your organisation's requirements.
- ❑ **Take corrective action** – where the actual or potential use of resources is significantly different from your plan, take appropriate action; this may mean altering activities, modifying the way you use resources or renegotiating your resource allocation.
- ❑ **Use resources efficiently** – and minimise any potential negative impact on the environment.
- ❑ **Improve your use of resources continuously** – always look for ways of using resources more efficiently, and implement any changes promptly.
- ❑ **Keep accurate records of resource usage** – these will help you identify problems and plan the use of resources better in the future.

Managing budgets

This section is about making sure projects and operations meet their financial targets.

The checklists will help you to

■ prepare estimates of income and expenditure based on the best information available
■ negotiate effectively with those who have to agree the budget
■ regularly check on performance against budget and make modifications where appropriate.

The process for *Managing budgets* looks like this.

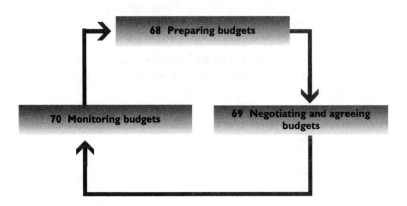

Preparing budgets

❑ **Prepare accurate estimates of benefits, income and costs –** base your estimates on valid, reliable information, with historical data and trends where available.

❑ **Assess alternative courses of action –** before submitting your budget and recommending expenditure assess the relative benefits and costs of alternative courses of action.

❑ **Encourage team members to contribute to the budget –** if team members are involved in the process of drawing up the budget, they will be more committed to achieving the benefits and income and keeping costs within agreed limits.

❑ **Indicate the benefits clearly –** be sure to specify the net benefit which will be gained, over time, from the expenditure.

❑ **State your assumptions –** make it clear what assumptions you have made and why.

❑ **Allow for contingencies –** take into account future changes which may affect the level of income and expenditure.

❑ **Check your budgets with others –** where other people have been involved in providing information or making suggestions, check the details with them before submitting your final budget.

❑ **Present your budget clearly and concisely –** make use of any forms which your organisation may have developed for presenting budgets.

❑ **Be prepared to give a fuller explanation –** have all your information and arguments to hand to counter challenges to your proposed budget.

❑ **Learn from your experience –** compare actual costs and benefits with the budget and use this information to help you improve your budgeting in the future.

❑ **Prepare people in advance** – involve team members, colleagues and those who will be agreeing the budgets in discussing assumptions and drawing up the budgets.

❑ **State your assumptions and the contingencies allowed for** – make it clear what assumptions you have made and what contingencies you have anticipated.

❑ **Present your budget clearly and concisely** – make use of any forms your organisation may have developed for presenting budgets and emphasise the benefits to your organisation.

❑ **Be as accurate as you can in your estimates** – use all the information available to support your calculations.

❑ **Allow sufficient time for negotiation** – present your budget sufficiently early to allow you to provide further information if required.

❑ **Negotiate with a spirit of good-will** – show that you intend to find a mutually acceptable solution.

❑ **Seek clarification where there is uncertainty or disagreement** – ask relevant people for guidance and help in finding an acceptable solution.

❑ **Communicate the budget decisions** – tell all those with an interest in the outcomes of budget negotiations about the decisions promptly, in order to secure their support, co-operation and confidence.

70 Monitoring budgets

❑ **Get people involved** – encourage your team members to take individual and collective responsibility to control activities against budgets.

❑ **Check actual income and expenditure against budgets** – get accurate information on revenue and costs at appropriate intervals.

❑ **Keep expenditure within agreed limits** – be clear what your budget limits are, make sure you keep within these and check that all expenditure conforms to your organisation's policies and procedures.

❑ **Phase expenditure according to a planned time scale** – make sure you do not overspend your budget in any period, even if you are still within budget for the year, as this will be detrimental to cash flow.

❑ **Report any likely over or under-spend against budget** – let the appropriate people know as soon as possible of any potential variance against budget.

❑ **Report any likely variance in income against budget** – let the appropriate people know as soon as possible if income is likely to be under or over budget.

❑ **Give the reasons for any variances** – analyse the causes for variances in income or expenditure and propose corrective action.

❑ **Take prompt corrective action** – take appropriate action where there are actual or potential significant deviations from budget.

❑ **Get authority for changes in allocations between budget heads** – where you need to spend more in one budget head and less in another, obtain any necessary authorisation from the appropriate people.

❑ **Get approval for changes to budgets** – where you need to change your budget during the accounting period, get approval from the appropriate people.

Controlling finances

This section is about managing the finances of your organisation, or your part of the organisation, in order to achieve the best possible financial outcome.

The checklists will help you to

- keep tight control on expenditure
- ensure you have sufficient cash to fund your on-going activities
- reduce the incidence of bad debts to a minimum.

The process of **Controlling finances** looks like this.

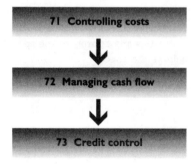

71 Controlling costs

↓

72 Managing cash flow

↓

73 Credit control

71 Controlling costs

❏ **Make every member of your team aware of how they can help to control costs** – get them to consider areas where costs could be reduced and bring to their attention costs they could help to reduce.

❏ **Keep expenditure within agreed budgets** – know what your budget limits are and check that you keep within them.

❏ **Where expenditure is outside your responsibility, refer requests promptly to the appropriate people** – many costs are the responsibility of another department; let them know promptly if you need their authorisation for expenditure.

❏ **Keep records of expenditure** – keep accurate and complete records available for reference.

❏ **Carefully assess information on costs and the use of resources** – regular reviews of costs will help you identify areas where these can be reduced or resources better utilised.

❏ **Look for improvements** – make recommendations for efficiency improvements as quickly as possible to the appropriate people.

❏ **Take prompt corrective action** – where expenditure is likely to exceed budget, report this immediately to the appropriate people and take action to minimise the effects.

Managing cash flow

❑ **Prepare a cash flow forecast** – get full information on expected receipts and payments to determine the likely pattern of cash flows over the accounting period.

❑ **Consider all the factors** – these may include regular receipts and payments, capital receipts and payments, drawings, dividends and disbursements and exceptional receipts and payments.

❑ **Present cash budgets** – present your budgets in the approved format, clearly indicating the net cash required for each period.

❑ **Monitor receipts and payments** – monitor cash receipts and payments regularly against budgeted cash flow.

❑ **Take prompt corrective action** – in the event of significant actual or potential deviations from the cash budget, take appropriate action such as arranging overdraft facilities, investing surplus cash or expediting debt collection.

❑ **Manage your cash balances** – anticipate surpluses and deficits and take appropriate action, taking into account trends in the financial or economic environment.

❑ **Invest surplus funds** – invest any surplus funds in marketable securities, in line with your organisation's financial procedures and authorisation limits.

❑ **Arrange overdraft or loan facilities where required** – anticipate the need for an overdraft or loan and get the most favourable terms possible, in line with your organisation's financial procedures.

❑ **Maintain an adequate level of liquidity** – keep sufficient cash readily available to meet known requirements and possible contingencies.

❑ **Maintain security of cash** – always observe your organisation's financial regulations and security procedures when handling cash.

73 Credit control

❑ **Establish and comply with your organisation's credit policy –** ensure you comply with your organisation's policy whenever you agree credit terms with customers.

❑ **Run credit checks on current and potential customers –** use valid information sources to ensure your customers are credit-worthy.

❑ **Only open new accounts for customers with an established credit status.**

❑ **Present invoices promptly –** send invoices to your customers on the agreed date, clearly specifying the credit terms agreed.

❑ **Monitor your debtors' accounts regularly –** analyse key indicators such as the age analysis of debtors, the average periods of credit given and received and the incidence of bad and doubtful debts.

❑ **Provide information about debtors' accounts –** tell relevant people in your organisation about significant outstanding accounts and potential bad debts, and recommend the action which should be taken.

❑ **Recover the monies owing to your organisation –** use debt recovery methods which are appropriate to individual cases and in line with your organisation's policies and procedures.

❑ **Deal with debtors firmly and courteously.**

❑ **Write off bad or doubtful debts only after weighing up all known factors.**

❑ **Use external agencies and advisers –** where appropriate, use outside specialists, such as debt collection or factoring agencies or lawyers, to implement your credit control policies effectively.

Selecting suppliers

This section is about selecting suppliers for any commodity, product or service.

The checklists will help you

- draw up a list of potential suppliers
- obtain bids or tenders which can be evaluated accurately and fairly
- clarify any points in offers which are unclear
- improve on these offers where possible
- select the most appropriate supplier.

The process of **Selecting suppliers** looks like this.

74 Selecting potential suppliers

❑ **Identify potential suppliers** – make sure you draw up your list of potential suppliers in line with organisational policy and legal requirements.

❑ **Develop selection criteria for those invited to quote** – in line with organisational policy and legal requirements.

❑ **Invite potential suppliers to quote** – make sure the number and range of suppliers is in line with organisational policy and legal requirements appropriate for specified supplies.

❑ **Establish selection criteria for the successful supplier** – in line with organisational policy and legal requirements.

Obtaining bids 75

❑ **Draw up a clear specification** – check that it conforms to relevant legal requirements.

❑ **Invite potential suppliers to bid against the specification.**

❑ **Ask for bids in a standard format** – this will allow for easy comparison of bids.

❑ **Be clear about the procedures and timetable for submitting bids** – check that these procedures are followed.

❑ **Resolve queries from potential suppliers promptly.**

76 Obtaining tenders

☐ **Draw up tender documents** – in line with organisational policy and legal requirements.

☐ **State the specification of supplies and conditions of contract** – state specifications clearly and accurately.

☐ **Give full information on procedures for submission of tenders.**

☐ **Advertise the tender** – in line with organisational policy and legal requirements.

☐ **Obtain sufficient tenders** – make sure that adequate competition has been secured.

☐ **Receive, record and open tenders** – following organisational procedures and legal requirements.

☐ **Resolve queries from suppliers who are tendering promptly and fairly.**

Clarifying and improving offers

❑ **Promptly resolve any queries over variances from specification** – in line with organisational policy and contract terms and conditions.

❑ **Obtain advice on any variances from specification** – ask users and technical staff about the implications of any variances.

❑ **Raise any queries relating to conditions of supply promptly** – clarify the situation with the supplier and record it accurately.

❑ **Consult between users, suppliers and purchasers** – in line with organisational policy and professional requirements.

❑ **Determine the scope and content of any negotiation** – this may well be constrained by the method of obtaining the offer.

❑ **Negotiate improvements to conditions of supply and confirm these with the supplier** – conditions of supply may include price, quantity, quality standards, carriage and delivery, maintenance and after-sales service, method of payment and terms of payment.

78   Deciding on supplier

❑ **Evaluate offers against established criteria –** in line with organisational policy and legal requirements.

❑ **Fully document your decision and reasons for this decision.**

❑ **Communicate your decision promptly –** to users, suppliers and other interested parties.

❑ **Use performance rating accurately in the selection of suppliers –** if you are using a system of rating the performance of suppliers, use this accurately and fairly.

Contracting for supply

This section is about finalising a contract for the supply of any commodity, product or service.

The checklists will help you to

- negotiate a valid contract with conditions which are advantageous to your organisation
- establish clear, agreed and legally-binding terms within the contract
- place the contract with your chosen supplier
- deal with any claims arising from the contract
- resolve any problems arising from the contract.

The process for **Contracting for supply** looks like this.

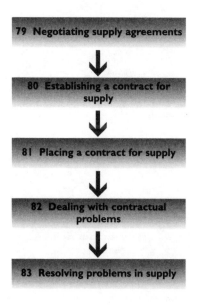

79 Negotiating supply agreements

↓

80 Establishing a contract for supply

↓

81 Placing a contract for supply

↓

82 Dealing with contractual problems

↓

83 Resolving problems in supply

79 Negotiating supply agreements

- ❏ **Ensure that the supply agreement meets established criteria.**
- ❏ **Ensure that the supply agreement conforms with organisational policy and legal requirements.**
- ❏ **Ensure that the negotiation results in savings to your organisation.**
- ❏ **Conduct negotiations in a professional manner.**
- ❏ **Evaluate the results of negotiations against your objectives –** and learn from your experience.
- ❏ **Agree arrangements for the management of supply agreement –** with both suppliers and users.

Establishing a contract for supply ⏹ 80

❑ **Ensure the contract is valid and legally binding.**

❑ **Seek appropriate legal advice where necessary –** and act upon it.

❑ **Ensure the contract offers adequate protection and acceptable risk regarding any possible breach of contract.**

❑ **Clearly establish criteria for determining failure to supply –** and state the agreed remedies within the contract.

81 | Placing a contract for supply

- ❑ **Complete the contract accurately** – include all necessary information.
- ❑ **Send the completed contract to the supplier** – adhere to agreed targets, budgets and time scales.
- ❑ **Obtain approval for the contract from the person with designated authority.**
- ❑ **Resolve any queries on the contract promptly** – and provide feedback to user and supplier.
- ❑ **Send the contract via the means agreed.**
- ❑ **Obtain appropriate acknowledgement of receipt** – of the contract and approval of its content.
- ❑ **Distribute copies of the contract** – to users and other designated staff.

Dealing with contractual problems 82

❏ **Investigate any claims** – establish whether they are valid or not.

❏ **Clarify any queries on claims promptly with contracting parties.**

❏ **Seek appropriate legal advice** – and act upon it when necessary.

❏ **Document claims accurately.**

❏ **Communicate the reasons for the claim** – tell relevant parties promptly the circumstances which gave rise to the claim.

❏ **Refer claims to the designated person** – if the claim is outside your authority.

83 **Resolving problems in supply**

❏ **Tell suppliers promptly about any complaints by users.**

❏ **Identify the cause of the problem.**

❏ **Discuss the problem quickly –** try to resolve the problem promptly by discussing it with suppliers and users.

❏ **Tell someone in authority about the problem.**

❏ **Seek legal advice on the problem if necessary.**

❏ **Obtain alternative supplies –** if the problem results in failure to supply.

❏ **Take action to redress the unsatisfactory supply –** take appropriate action according to the terms of the contract.

❏ **Negotiate any alterations to terms and method of payment with suppliers and users –** and record these accurately.

❏ **Take action to ensure that future supplies will meet user specification.**

❏ **Record problems and how they were resolved –** tell users about them and include these in your appraisal of your supplier's performance.

→ Managing energy

This section is about making sure you use energy resources (such as electricity, gas, oil or coal) as efficiently as possible.

The checklists will help you to

- assess the energy performance of your organisation, or the part for which you are responsible
- make sure that your plans and working practices use energy as efficiently as possible
- continuously improve your energy performance.

The process for **Managing energy** looks like this.

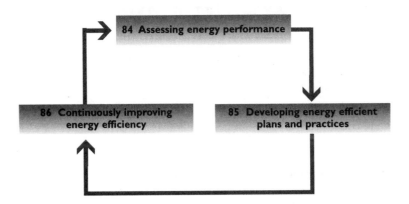

84 | **Assessing energy performance**

❑ **Get people involved** – encourage appropriate colleagues and members of your team to contribute to assessing energy performance.

❑ **Identify appropriate measures, tools and techniques** – choose performance measures and assessment tools and techniques which allow you to evaluate energy usage accurately.

❑ **Obtain sufficient information** – make sure you have sufficient, relevant information on a regular basis to allow you to make an accurate and complete assessment.

❑ **Investigate any weaknesses, confusions or discrepancies in the information** – and take appropriate action to get information of the quality you require.

❑ **Record information carefully** – store complete and accurate information according to organisational requirements.

❑ **Base your assessments and forecasts on relevant information** – make all your criteria and assumptions clear in your report.

❑ **Report on your energy performance on a regular basis** – and make sure these reports are received by the appropriate people and provide sufficient information for them to take decisions.

❑ **Identify areas for improvement** – compare your energy performance with current best practice and with technological developments.

❑ **Evaluate opportunities to improve energy efficiency** – weigh up the advantages and disadvantages (such as safety, cost, reliability, environment, quality) in relation to your organisation's systems and practices.

❑ **Make recommendations for improvement** – make realistic recommendations for improving your energy efficiency in line with your organisation's energy management strategies and policies.

Developing energy efficient plans and practices

❑ **Seek specialist advice** – when developing your plans and working practices, get specialist advice on how to use energy more efficiently.

❑ **Set targets for energy performance** – include clear targets for energy usage in your plans.

❑ **Choose the most energy efficient resources** – select and use resources (such as finance, people, premises, equipment, materials and energy supplies) which make the best use of energy.

❑ **Adopt energy efficient practices** – use the most energy efficient practices consistent with meeting your work objectives and with the resources you have available.

❑ **Encourage people to evaluate and improve working practices** – get your team members to evaluate the effects of their own working practices on energy performance and take action to improve these practices, if appropriate.

❑ **Monitor changes in working practices** – evaluate the effects and whether changes in working practices really lead to improved energy performance.

❑ **Monitor the use of energy** – monitor whether targeted energy performance is achieved in the implementation of your plans.

❑ **Take corrective action where necessary** – where targeted energy performance is not achieved, take appropriate action to amend your plans or working practices.

86 Continuously improving energy efficiency

❑ **Encourage people to identify opportunities** – which improve energy efficiency and contribute to the effective use of energy and a sustainable environment.

❑ **Regularly review current resources, systems and activities** – look for opportunities to improve energy efficiency.

❑ **Identify developments and advances in best practice in the wider environment** – see if any new products, services, technological innovations or innovative working practices could help improve your energy efficiency.

❑ **Check the validity of monitoring and analytical techniques** – make sure your techniques for monitoring and analysing energy usage allow you to spot opportunities for improvements.

❑ **Assess the results of monitoring, evaluations and audits** – what are their implications for your organisation's activities?

❑ **Communicate the results of monitoring** – let people know how energy efficient they are, and how their performance could be improved.

❑ **Evaluate potential improvements** – weigh up the advantages of potential improvements against any investment costs for your organisation.

❑ **Implement improvements** – where improvements are cost-effective, implement them promptly and encourage people to support these improvements.

CHAPTER 4

Manage information

Manage information is about ensuring prompt access to information in order to make decisions.

Establishing information management and communication systems

This section is about establishing and monitoring systems to provide the right information and to communicate this as effectively as possible.

The checklists will help you to

- identify the information you need
- identify how information should flow within your organisation and with the outside world
- choose the best information and communication management systems for your needs
- implement these systems effectively in your organisation
- check that the systems are working effectively and deal with any problems arising.

The process of establishing and maintaining effective **Information management and communication systems** looks like this.

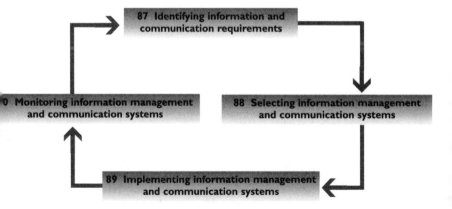

87 | Identifying information and communication requirements

- ❑ **Consult with those who will be using the systems** – ask those inside and outside your organisation who will be using the systems, or affected by them, about their requirements.

- ❑ **Research information requirements** – consider the following
  - the range of information required
  - the level of detail required
  - the purpose to which it will be put
  - who needs to access it, how, and how quickly
  - legal and statutory requirements
  - the requirements for confidentiality and restrictions on access.

- ❑ **Research communication processes** – how does information flow within your organisation and between the organisation and your outside world? What media, processes and systems are likely to be used in the future?

- ❑ **Specify information and communication requirements** – agree these in detail with users.

- ❑ **Specify the resources required** – and get authority for these resources.

- ❑ **Be consistent** – check your specifications are consistent with your organisation's objectives, values and policies.

Selecting information management and communication systems

❏ **Agree the criteria for selection of information management and communication systems** – draw up clear criteria and agree these with users and others involved or affected by the systems.

❏ **Evaluate viable systems** – only consider systems which are capable of meeting your requirements within your budget.

❏ **Weigh up the benefits and disadvantages** – carefully assess the pros and cons of all viable systems.

❏ **Select the best system for your purposes** – choose the system which most closely meets your criteria.

❏ **Develop an implementation plan** – agree your detailed plan for implementing the new system with users and others involved or affected by the system.

89 | Implementing information management and communication systems

❑ **Present your plan** – share your plan for implementing the new information management and communication system with users and others involved or affected by the system.

❑ **Get people involved** – encourage users and others involved to make effective and creative contributions to the implementation process.

❑ **Check people's understanding** – check that users and others involved understand the planned system and their role in its implementation.

❑ **Sell the benefits** – gain people's support by specifying the benefits of the new systems, both for the organisation and for the individuals within it.

❑ **Get sufficient resources** – make sure you have sufficient resources to allow the implementation to take place within the agreed time scales.

❑ **Monitor the implementation** – check that the milestones and staged targets in your plans are being met.

❑ **Modify your plans as appropriate** – if there are any problems, take action to resolve them.

❑ **Deliver on time** – implement the new system on time, within budget and to the specification agreed.

Monitoring information management and communication systems
90

❑ **Get users involved** – encourage users to provide feedback on the effectiveness and performance of the information management and communication systems.

❑ **Monitor the systems regularly** – establish and follow formal monitoring procedures and evaluate the performance of systems against agreed measures and criteria.

❑ **Take account of trends and developments** – look for trends in performance in order to anticipate problems, and developments in technology which may help you solve the problems or enhance your systems.

❑ **Deal with problems** – modify systems appropriately to overcome any problems identified.

❑ **Gain support for improvements** – present the results of monitoring and evaluations, and your recommendations for improvements to system design or usage, in a way which attracts the support of users and others involved in or affected by the systems.

Using information

This section is about obtaining, using and presenting information to aid decision-making.

The checklists will help you to

- identify and obtain the information you need
- record and store information in a way which makes it easy to retrieve
- analyse and evaluate the value of information
- use information to forecast future trends and developments
- take decisions which are complex or critical to your organisation
- present information and provide advice to others.

The process of *Using information* looks like this.

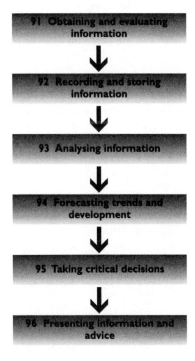

91 Obtaining and evaluating information

❑ **Identify what information you require** – regularly consider the kind of information you are going to need.

❑ **Review your sources of information** – regularly review a wide range of sources of information and consider how useful, reliable and cost-effective they are.

❑ **Develop your networks** – establish, maintain and develop contacts with people who may be able to provide you with useful information.

❑ **Seek out all relevant information** – make sure you have information on all relevant factors affecting current or potential operations.

❑ **Try alternative ways of getting information** – if you are having trouble getting information from one source, try a different route in or an alternative source.

❑ **Get clear information** – if the information you have is ambiguous or contradictory, challenge it until the information is clear and accurate.

❑ **Collect information in time for it to be of use** – make sure information arrives before the deadline.

❑ **Present information in a suitable form to aid decision-making** – use summaries, diagrams and recommendations to help decision-making.

❑ **Draw appropriate conclusions** – make sure your conclusions are fully supported by the relevant information and reasoned argument.

❑ **Review your methods of obtaining information** – review your methods on a regular basis and improve them where necessary.

Recording and storing information

❑ **Record information accurately** – check the quality of records.

❑ **Record information in appropriate detail** – you will need to keep a different level of detail on information, depending on how significant it is and how you anticipate using it.

❑ **Record and store information using accepted formats, systems and procedures** – your organisation may have developed formal procedures and systems for storing different types of information, both paper-based and on computer.

❑ **Make sure you can retrieve information promptly when required** – consider how urgently the information may be needed.

❑ **Review your methods for recording and storing information** – re-evaluate your methods, systems and procedures on a regular basis to check that they are as effective and efficient as possible.

❑ **Introduce new methods of recording and storing information as needed** – regularly review whether the supply of information continues to meet requirements.

❑ **Analyse and correct any breakdowns in the methods of recording and storing information** – when systems do breakdown, analyse the cause, and take action to ensure similar breakdowns do not re-occur.

❑ **Comply with legal requirements** – ensure your systems for recording, storing and providing information meet the legal and organisational requirements for confidentiality.

Analysing information

❏ **Be clear about the objectives** – ask the question: what are the objectives of the analysis and what decisions need to be made?

❏ **Select appropriate information** – get accurate information which is relevant to the objectives of the analysis and sufficient to arrive at a reliable decision.

❏ **Choose appropriate methods** – use methods which are suitable to achieve the objectives of the analysis.

❏ **Identify patterns and trends from the information.**

❏ **Draw conclusions from the analysis** – make sure these are supported by reasoned argument and appropriate evidence.

❏ **Differentiate between fact and opinion** – when presenting the results of your analysis, make it clear what is fact and what is your opinion or interpretation.

❏ **Keep complete records** – provide an audit trail of the assumptions and decisions made at each stage of the analysis.

Forecasting trends and developments

❏ **Base your forecasts on the best information available** – make sure you are using the best information given the constraints of time and cost.

❏ **Make your forecasts of trends and developments at an appropriate time** – you will need to make some forecasts prior to planning; other developments may require forecasts to be regularly updated.

❏ **Provide suitable quantitative information for decision-making** – include in your forecasts sufficient quantitative information to allow you, and your colleagues, to be able to make decisions about allocating resources.

❏ **State the assumptions underlying your forecasts** – clearly state your assumptions and the reasons for them.

❏ **State the degree of certainty of your forecasts** – highlight those areas which are most at risk or where there is little evidence to support your forecast.

❏ **Illustrate the impact of trends and developments** – show how these trends will affect operations and the achievement of organisational objectives.

❏ **Review your forecasts** – analyse the reasons for any inaccuracies in your forecasts, and use this information to improve future forecasts.

95 **Taking critical decisions**

❑ **Involve others in decision-making** – think who could usefully contribute to the decision-making process (colleagues, team members, higher-level managers or specialists), and consult with them in time for their views to be taken into account.

❑ **Base your decisions on reliable information** – make sure you have sufficient qualitative and quantitative information on which to base your decisions and that your analysis of this information is valid.

❑ **Assess the risks** – where there is incomplete or contradictory information, assess the likelihood of events not turning out as anticipated, in order to understand, and minimise, the risks involved.

❑ **Take decisions which are consistent** – are they consistent with previous decisions, and with organisational values, policies, guidelines and procedures?

❑ **Obtain advice from relevant people** – get help from others if you have insufficient information or if your decisions are likely to conflict with organisational values, policies, guidelines or procedures.

❑ **Take decisions in good time** – make sure you take decisions in time for appropriate action to be taken.

❑ **Communicate your decisions** – think about all those who need to know about the decision, and make sure they are informed clearly and promptly.

❑ **Review your decisions** – periodically review the results of your decisions and the process by which they were taken in order to improve decision-making in the future.

Presenting information and advice

❑ **Communicate** – seize opportunities to disseminate information and advice.

❑ **Make sure your information is current, relevant and accurate** – prepare carefully what you are going to say and check it with colleagues or specialists.

❑ **Maintain confidentiality** – make sure that you do not divulge information which is confidential.

❑ **Check that your advice is consistent with organisational policy** – check with colleagues or specialists to ensure you are providing accurate advice.

❑ **Support your advice** – where appropriate, provide reasoned argument and evidence to support your advice.

❑ **Think about your audience** – put yourself in your audience's position, think what information they need, and present it in a manner, and at a level and pace which is appropriate.

❑ **Check that your audience has understood** – ask questions, or use feedback, to check your audience has understood the information presented.

❑ **Improve your presentations** – use feedback from your audience to improve the way you present information and advice.

Meetings

This section is about leading and participating in meetings to make decisions.

The checklists will help you to

- be clear about the purpose of the meeting and make sure its objectives are achieved
- prepare and make your contributions effectively
- encourage contributions from all participants
- take decisions.

This section covers

> **97 Leading meetings**

> **98 Participating in meetings**

Leading meetings

❏ **Be clear about the purpose of the meeting** – do not call a meeting if there is a better way to exchange information, consult with people, solve a problem or make a decision.

❏ **Invite the appropriate people to attend** – only invite those people who have something to contribute or gain, but make sure you invite all the people necessary to take decisions.

❏ **Allow time for preparation** – carefully prepare how you will lead the meeting and talk to other members; circulate papers in advance so everyone can be well prepared.

❏ **State the purpose of the meeting at the outset** – check that all those attending understand the reasons for which they are present.

❏ **Allocate sufficient time** – set a fixed time for the meeting to begin and end and allocate time appropriately for each item under discussion.

❏ **Encourage all present to contribute** – use questions and individual encouragement to ensure all views are represented.

❏ **Discourage unhelpful comments and digressions** – be firm, but sensitive, in asking those present to keep to the purpose of the meeting.

❏ **Summarise** – summarise the discussion at appropriate times and allocate action points at the end of each item.

❏ **Take decisions** – make sure that decisions are within the meeting's authority, that they are accurately recorded and promptly communicated to those who need to know.

❏ **Evaluate the meeting** – allow time at the end of the meeting to evaluate whether the purpose of the meeting has been effectively achieved.

Participating in meetings

❏ **Prepare carefully** – get any papers or information in advance, and consult with others whom you are representing, so you can prepare how best to contribute to the meeting.

❏ **Contribute effectively** – present your contributions clearly, accurately and at the appropriate time.

❏ **Help to solve problems** – think about how you can help identify and clarify problems and suggest solutions which will help the meeting to arrive at a valid decision.

❏ **Keep to the point** – remember what the purpose of the meeting is and do not digress.

❏ **Acknowledge the contributions and viewpoints of others** – acknowledge others' contributions and discuss these constructively, even if you disagree with them.

❏ **Represent your group effectively** – if you are at the meeting as the representative of your organisation, department or team, make sure you fully represent their views, not just your own.

❏ **Follow up your action points** – make a note of the points you need to action and make sure you do so within the agreed time scale.

❏ **Communicate decisions and information** – inform those who need to know about the decisions of the meeting, but keep confidential information confidential.

PART 2

Strategic management

What is strategic management?

Senior managers need to be excellent operational managers, but they also need to have the skills to develop and implement strategies to further their organisation's mission. Strategic management is about charting the direction for the organisation and ensuring it stays on course towards its goals.

Members of the organisation's board or governing body, and those reporting to them, will devote much of their time to strategic management, as well as fulfilling their functional or operational role. Depending on the size or structure of the organisation, relatively junior managers may also play an important part in strategic management.

Strategic management requires a sound understanding of the environment in which your organisation is working. You must be aware of what is happening in the external environment in which you operate and seize opportunities to influence this environment in your favour. You also need an objective view of your own organisation's strengths and weaknesses. You need to provide clear leadership and a vision for your organisation, and get all parties to agree to your mission, values, policies and objectives.

From the strategic objectives are developed the programmes, projects and operating plans which are delegated to contractors or operational managers to achieve. These contractors and operational managers will need your continual guidance and support as well as monitoring to ensure they are achieving their objectives in a way which is consistent with your organisation's culture and values.

The cycle of strategic management is completed with a review of your organisation's performance, a reappraisal of its mission, policies and objectives and a search for ways of doing things better in the future. The cycle of strategic management is continuous and complex with many feedback loops and links into the operational role. The checklists on the following pages have been designed to be clear, practical guidelines for carrying out the tasks of strategic management.

CHAPTER 5

Reviewing the environment

Reviewing the environment is about understanding your own organisation's strengths and weaknesses in the environment in which you are working so that you can develop the most effective strategy.

Reviewing the external environment

This section is about identifying the opportunities and threats in the external environment in which you operate.

The checklists will help you to

■ develop cost-effective systems for reviewing your markets
■ influence and respond to the political and trading environments
■ identify the strengths and weaknesses of other players, competitors and collaborators.

The process of *Reviewing the external environment* looks like this.

99 Researching your markets

100 Responding to the political and trading environment

101 Identifying competitors and partners

Researching your markets

❑ **Develop cost-effective systems for reviewing market possibilities** – choose systems and techniques which cost-effectively identify opportunities to provide your services or products.

❑ **Use field-intelligence** – get your own employees and agents to provide relevant information on customer needs.

❑ **Use customer feedback** – encourage your customers to tell you what they think about your products and services and what they will want from you in the future.

❑ **Get comprehensive market analyses** – make sure the information you have on the market is up-to-date, well-evidenced and accurately reflects the current and predicted trends.

❑ **Take into account possible future interests and activities** – your market review must be forward-looking, taking into account the future interests and activities of your organisation, its partners and competitors.

❑ **Define your market as broadly as possible** – do not take a too narrow, traditional view of your market, but recognise the opportunities for diversity and diversification.

Responding to the political and trading environment

❑ **Develop cost-effective systems for gathering information –** choose systems and techniques which cost-effectively identify actual or potential opportunities and threats in the political, regulatory and trading environment.

❑ **Use field-intelligence –** get your own employees and agents to provide relevant information on changes in the environment.

❑ **Use customer and supplier feedback –** encourage customers and suppliers to discuss with you how they see the environment changing.

❑ **Get comprehensive analyses of the environment –** make sure the information you have on the environment is up-to-date, backed by good evidence and accurately reflects the current and predicted trends.

❑ **Take into account possible future interests and activities –** your review of the environment must be forward-looking, taking into account the future interests and activities of your organisation, its partners and competitors.

❑ **Seize opportunities to change the external environment –** take opportunities to change the environment in your interests and to influence key opinion-formers and decision-makers.

❑ **Use ethical methods to influence the environment –** make sure the methods you and your employees use to influence the external environment are ethical, consistent with your organisation's values and sensitive to the values of stakeholders.

❑ **Be clear about the constraints imposed by the external environment –** understand what the constraints are and what their implications are for your organisation.

101 Identifying competitors and partners

❑ **Develop cost-effective systems for evaluating competitors and partners** – choose systems and techniques which cost-effectively identify the strengths and weaknesses of existing and potential competitors and partners.

❑ **Use field-intelligence** – get your own employees and agents to provide relevant information on competitors and partners.

❑ **Use customer and supplier feedback** – encourage customers and suppliers to provide you with information on the activities of competitors and partners.

❑ **Evaluate the strengths and weaknesses of your competitors and partners** – make sure your evaluation is based on up-to-date information and reflects current and predicted trends.

❑ **Take into account possible future interests and activities** – your review should take account of the future interests and activities of your organisation, its competitors and partners.

❑ **Use ethical methods** – make sure the methods you use to identify and evaluate competitors and partners are ethical, consistent with your organisation's values and sensitive to the values of your stakeholders.

❑ **Adjust your plans** – amend your plans in the light of information on competitors and partners.

❑ **Set comparative targets** – as well as your internal targets, set targets which compare your performance with that of your competitors.

❑ **Develop the case for partnership** – where a partnership seems possible, develop a case which is backed by good evidence, acceptable in terms of the risk involved and consistent with the future plans of your organisation.

Reviewing your organisation

This section is about identifying the strengths and weaknesses of your own organisation.

The checklists will help you to

- review the strengths and weaknesses of your products and services
- look for ways of improving your organisation's structures
- identify the strengths and weaknesses of the management team
- develop the management team
- review how you acquire and allocate financial resources.

The process of *Reviewing your organisation* looks like this.

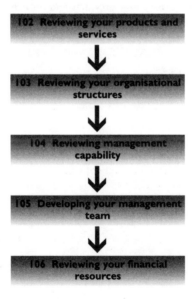

102 Reviewing your products and services

⬇

103 Reviewing your organisational structures

⬇

104 Reviewing management capability

⬇

105 Developing your management team

⬇

106 Reviewing your financial resources

102 **Reviewing your products and services**

❏ **Undertake a regular review** – review your organisation's products and services regularly, at least once per year.

❏ **Identify problems and opportunities for products and services** – look at both internal and external factors which may present problems or opportunities for your products and services.

❏ **Use all available information** – use both quantitative and qualitative data to help identify problems and opportunities.

❏ **Use employee and customer feedback** – encourage staff and customers to discuss potential problems and opportunities.

❏ **Be rigorous and imaginative in your diagnosis** – get right to the essential cause of any problem and consider a range of other possible causes.

❏ **Focus on solutions** – having diagnosed the problem accurately, consider how to improve your product or service or your organisation's operations.

❏ **Search for new ideas** – use creative thinking techniques to identify opportunities to develop new products and services.

Reviewing your organisational structures | 103

❏ **Undertake regular reviews** – review your organisational structure and communication systems regularly, but avoid continual restructuring if possible.

❏ **Identify obstacles and opportunities in organisational structures and communication systems** – look at both the internal and external factors which may present obstacles or opportunities.

❏ **Solicit suggestions from staff** – encourage all staff to suggest ways of improving structures and systems.

❏ **Consult on proposed improvements** – consult with all those affected by changes to structures and systems in time for their views to be taken into account.

❏ **Justify proposed improvements** – base your proposals for improvements on hard facts.

❏ **Take into account the needs and expectations of stakeholders** – research stakeholders needs and expectations and modify proposals accordingly.

❏ **Communicate the practical requirements** – make sure all those affected know what they are required to do to implement the improvements.

❏ **Implement improvements in a timely manner** – make sure that you take action in sufficient time to be able to meet the new circumstances.

❏ **Monitor improvements** – check that the improvements are delivering the benefits you expected.

104   Reviewing management capability

❑ **Identify and evaluate the strengths and weaknesses of your management team** – ensure your assessments are clear, unambiguous and fair.

❑ **Choose appropriate techniques** – select identification and evaluation techniques which meet your information needs.

❑ **Acknowledge the potential of managers from diverse backgrounds and experience** – develop a mix of different skills and experience in your team.

❑ **Present a balanced view** – where weaknesses are identified, present these in a balanced way, also taking into account strengths and potential.

❑ **Share your findings with your management team** – share your evaluation of the capability of your management team with team members, paying due regard to personal feelings and issues of confidentiality.

❑ **Carry out the assessments in time** – make sure the assessments are available in time to support decisions on the structure and development of the management team.

❑ **Consider the future** – when reviewing the capability of your management team, consider both current and future circumstances and needs.

Developing your management team

❑ **Be fair in the recruitment, selection and removal of managers** – make sure your policy and practice for the recruitment, selection and removal of managers is fair, ethical, legal and consistent with your organisation's values.

❑ **Share decisions on the development of the team** – involve the team in making decisions on their development, with due regard to personal feelings and issues of confidentiality.

❑ **Use suggestions of team members** – team members will be more committed to the development process if they have been consulted and their suggestions used wherever possible.

❑ **Consider a wide variety of development methods** – some methods may be more suited to the learning preferences of individuals in the team than others.

❑ **Take advantage of diverse backgrounds and experience** – in selecting development methods, take advantage of the racial, gender and social backgrounds of team members, and their varied experience.

❑ **Take advantage of different approaches and management styles** – in selecting development methods, take advantage of the various approaches which different managers or potential managers may take to the challenges facing your organisation.

❑ **Take advantage of skills within the team** – where members of the team have the necessary skills, provide opportunities for them to share these with other team members.

❑ **Choose cost-effective methods** – select those methods most likely to ensure managers are able to carry out their present and likely future roles.

❑ **Build on achievement** – recognise and build on existing achievements of managers and provide feedback on how their performance is developing.

Reviewing your financial resources

❏ **Develop systems to collect information –** you need information from those inside and outside your organisation who are responsible for acquiring and allocating financial resources.

❏ **Know who your friends are –** know as much as you can about all those who can either help or hinder the process of acquiring funds.

❏ **Judge your performance in context –** when selecting criteria for judging the performance of your organisation in acquiring and allocating funds, take into account the context and character of your organisation.

❏ **Use commonly accepted performance measures –** use commonly accepted measures which allow you to compare the performance of your organisation with others.

❏ **Make comparisons –** compare the performance of your organisation or units with that of other similar organisations.

❏ **Look at alternative means of financing –** compare your current performance with alternative means of acquisition and allocation of financial resources over short, medium and long-terms.

❏ **Take contingency action –** where your review reveals threats or opportunities, identify, communicate and implement alternative, feasible courses of action.

Stakeholders

This section is about identifying your stakeholders' interests and getting them on your side.

The checklists will help you to

- be clear about the interests of various groups of stakeholders
- develop a good relationship with your stakeholders
- secure their support and assistance.

This section covers

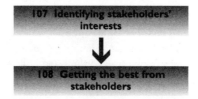

107 Identifying stakeholders' interests

108 Getting the best from stakeholders

107 Identifying stakeholders' interests

❑ **Be realistic and comprehensive, when identifying stakeholders' interests** – and take account of current and likely future activities of your organisation.

❑ **Use a wide range of methods to identify stakeholders' interests** – employ both quantitative and qualitative techniques.

❑ **Consult widely with people throughout your organisation** – use both formal and informal methods.

❑ **Use ethical methods** – and ensure that they are sensitive to racial, social and economic diversity.

❑ **Develop a relationship of trust with stakeholders** – consult with stakeholders in a way which generates their trust and leads to open expression of their interests.

❑ **Take account of stakeholders' interests** – modify your plans appropriately.

❑ **Take advantage of opportunities stakeholders provide** – show how stakeholders can help your organisation achieve its plans.

❑ **Acknowledge and resolve differences** – where stakeholders' interests appear to be based on a misunderstanding or are at variance with your organisation's objectives, values and policies, acknowledge these differences and try to resolve them.

❑ **Monitor and evaluate stakeholder reaction** – where an action is likely to excite particular or exceptional stakeholder interest, establish a way of monitoring and evaluation of the reaction.

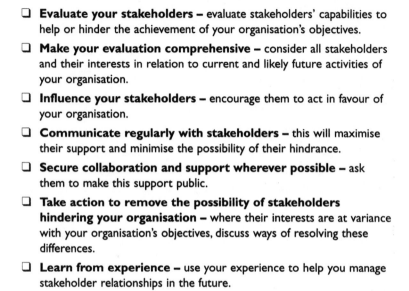

❑ **Evaluate your stakeholders** – evaluate stakeholders' capabilities to help or hinder the achievement of your organisation's objectives.

❑ **Make your evaluation comprehensive** – consider all stakeholders and their interests in relation to current and likely future activities of your organisation.

❑ **Influence your stakeholders** – encourage them to act in favour of your organisation.

❑ **Communicate regularly with stakeholders** – this will maximise their support and minimise the possibility of their hindrance.

❑ **Secure collaboration and support wherever possible** – ask them to make this support public.

❑ **Take action to remove the possibility of stakeholders hindering your organisation** – where their interests are at variance with your organisation's objectives, discuss ways of resolving these differences.

❑ **Learn from experience** – use your experience to help you manage stakeholder relationships in the future.

CHAPTER 6

Setting the strategy

Setting the strategy is about consulting all interested parties to decide the future direction and goals of your organisation and enlisting their support for your strategy.

Agreeing your strategy

This section is about developing, and gaining support for, your organisation's mission, values, policies and objectives.

The checklists will help you to

- consult widely with all stakeholders
- provide a vision for your organisation
- develop and agree your organisation's mission, values, policies and objectives
- gain support from your stakeholders.

The process of **Agreeing your strategy** looks like this.

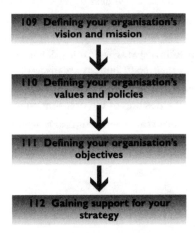

109 Defining your organisation's vision and mission

⬇

110 Defining your organisation's values and policies

⬇

111 Defining your organisation's objectives

⬇

112 Gaining support for your strategy

109 Defining your organisation's vision and mission

❏ **Consult with all stakeholders** – consult widely with all those individuals, groups and organisations (including customers, suppliers, employees and shareholders) who have an interest in the organisation to gain their views and suggestions.

❏ **Describe your organisation's role and ethos** – try to capture, in the mission statement, the ethos of your organisation and its role in the environment.

❏ **Make the mission both challenging and realistic** – check that the mission captures the aspirations of stakeholders and that these aspirations are achievable.

❏ **Encourage creativity, innovation and justifiable risk-taking** – frame the mission in a way which encourages innovative activity.

❏ **Discuss drafts of the mission statement with stakeholders** – explain the consequences and alternatives in order to gain their support.

❏ **Reflect stakeholders' views in the mission statement** – make sure the mission attracts the widest possible spectrum of support.

❏ **Keep the mission statement short and direct** – a single paragraph is normally enough to capture an organisation's mission.

❏ **Publish your mission statement** – it will help all members of your organisation focus their contributions creatively.

❏ **Provide a vision for the future** – frame the mission within an overall vision for the position of the organisation in the future.

❏ **Review the mission statement regularly** – up-date the mission in response to trends and opportunities.

Defining your organisation's values and policies | 110

❏ **Consult with stakeholders on the formulation of values and policies** – and incorporate their needs and ideas where possible.

❏ **Be consistent** – make sure your organisation's values and policies are consistent with its vision and mission.

❏ **Be realistic** – make sure your organisation's values and policies can be reflected in day-to-day work and working relationships.

❏ **Include guidance on dealing with difficult situations** – particularly how to respond when under pressure or when interests or policies are in conflict.

❏ **Be clear yet flexible** – make sure your values and policies are unambiguous yet allow people to respond and adhere to them in different ways.

❏ **Be comprehensive** – make sure your values and policies cover all aspects of your organisation's operations, its employees, representatives, suppliers and customers.

❏ **Publish your values and policies** – there is much to be gained in understanding and commitment if your organisation's values and policies are communicated to all stakeholders.

❏ **Keep up-to-date** – check regularly to ensure your values and policies are up-to-date and allow for likely future circumstances and issues.

Defining your organisation's objectives

❏ **Be consistent** – make sure your organisation's objectives are consistent with your mission and values.

❏ **Deliver the mission** – make sure that your objectives are capable of delivering your organisation's mission in an acceptable time scale and at an acceptable cost.

❏ **Be specific** – include sufficient detail to allow the development of specific programmes, projects and operating plans.

❏ **Acknowledge constraints** – clearly acknowledge and express any constraints upon objectives.

❏ **Define achievable and measurable objectives** – and state the types of measures and criteria to be used.

❏ **Consult with stakeholders** – hold open and realistic discussions about the objectives.

❏ **Revise objectives** – to meet actual or anticipated changes in circumstances.

Gaining support for your strategy

❏ **Consult and negotiate openly** – ensure that the mission, values, policies and objectives are influenced by and consistent with the interests of stakeholders.

❏ **Find the best balance of interests** – where interests of stakeholders are in conflict, find realistic and rational compromises which balance the interests and acknowledge the tensions.

❏ **Enlist stakeholders' support** – present the mission, values, policies and objectives to stakeholders in such a way as to attract their support.

❏ **Minimise any problems from lack of support** – where less than full support is achieved, identify the consequences and take action to minimise any problems.

❏ **Maintain regular consultation** – communicate regularly to ensure support is available when needed, especially in contingencies.

CHAPTER 7

Planning, implementation and control

Strategic managers need to help develop plans to realise the strategy, implement these plans through other managers or contractors and monitor the results.

Developing programmes, projects and plans

This section is about developing plans and securing agreement and support for them.

The checklists will help you to

- develop and submit proposals
- evaluate and amend proposals developed by others
- provide professional advice in developing proposals
- get the necessary support and resources to implement your plans
- gain approval for your plans.

The process for **Developing programmes, projects and plans** looks like this.

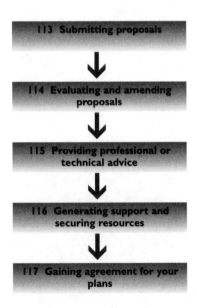

113 Submitting proposals

↓

114 Evaluating and amending proposals

↓

115 Providing professional or technical advice

↓

116 Generating support and securing resources

↓

117 Gaining agreement for your plans

113 Submitting proposals

❏ **Check that your proposals are consistent** – make sure they are consistent with your organisation's objectives and goals.

❏ **Consider the wider implications** – take into account other relevant programmes, projects and plans.

❏ **Make your proposals comprehensive and realistic** – provide appropriate information and analyses.

❏ **Draw together the range of relevant considerations** – incorporate in your proposals the operational, financial, legal, human resource, market and information considerations, as appropriate.

❏ **Present a clearly-argued rationale** – base your argument on valid information and organisational objectives.

❏ **Provide sufficient information** – present proposals with sufficient information to enable the target audience to evaluate them realistically.

❏ **Include measures of performance** – include in your proposals targets, standards and means of controlling their implementation.

❏ **Set out the method of implementation** – provide a timetable and budget, and allocate individual responsibility for the implementation of the proposal.

Evaluating and amending proposals 114

- ❏ **Establish a defined process for evaluating proposals** – clearly state the procedures, time scales and criteria involved, and stick to them.
- ❏ **Evaluate and amend proposals presented by others** – when evaluating proposals, take account of strategic objectives and the needs of your organisation as a whole.
- ❏ **Assess the benefits and costs** – judge proposals according to their expected benefits and costs and according to how realistic these benefits and costs appear, and always use a worst-case analysis.
- ❏ **Check consistency** – check that proposals are consistent with your organisation's objectives, plans, values and policies.
- ❏ **Check that the proposals take into account all relevant considerations** – including operational, financial, legal, human resource, market and information considerations.
- ❏ **Highlight any weaknesses or inconsistencies** – list these and point them out when rejecting proposals or asking for amendments.
- ❏ **Give reasons for rejecting proposals or referring them for amendment** – and offer help with preparing future proposals.

Providing professional or technical advice

❑ **Provide advice to help others prepare programmes, projects and plans** – provide advice either when requested or when it will improve the quality of strategic decisions.

❑ **Give evidence** – support your professional or technical advice with facts.

❑ **Distinguish opinion from advice** – make it clear when you are offering an opinion or personal preference rather than professional or technical advice.

❑ **Declare any conflict of interest** – where your own or your team's interests affect the advice offered, declare the potential conflict openly.

Generating support and securing resources 16

❏ **Generate support and secure resources for programmes, projects and plans** – communicate the benefits to those who control the resources.

❏ **Make a clear, unambiguous, consistent and supportable case** – present valid information in an appropriate format.

❏ **Be ethical and consistent** – ensure your activities to obtain support are ethical and consistent with the values and policies of your organisation.

❏ **Recognise the interests of stakeholders** – demonstrate how these are consistent with programmes, projects and plans.

❏ **Avoid undue risks** – avoid unacceptably hazardous relationships and potential damage to the good name of your organisation.

❏ **Exploit alliances and trade-offs** – use partnerships and be prepared to compromise as long as this does not risk producing negative consequences for your organisation.

❏ **Show commitment and drive** – reflect the commitment and drive of those who will be using the resources in the way you present your case.

117 Gaining agreement for your plans

❑ **Negotiate with the decision-makers** – ensure their support and agreement for your plans.

❑ **Satisfy all ethical, legal, value and policy requirements** – both in the way negotiations are conducted and in the way agreements are finalised.

❑ **Make concessions** – but only where these are consistent with the original intentions and with the objectives of the organisation.

❑ **Keep communication channels open at all times** – where agreement is not possible immediately, keep communication channels open whilst you obtain additional support, arguments or evidence.

❑ **Consider the wider implications of the agreement** – consider the wider implications for your organisation and carry out any necessary consultation.

Delegating and taking action

This section is about ensuring suppliers and staff can deliver the outcomes of plans.

The checklists will help you to

- negotiate contracts directly with suppliers
- delegate responsibility and authority to staff
- agree the objectives which have to be met
- provide on-going support and advice.

The process of **Delegation and taking action** looks like this.

118 Negotiating contracts with suppliers

❑ **Maintain a wide range of suppliers** – make sure you select from a sufficiently wide range of suppliers to encourage competition, diversity and innovation.

❑ **Negotiate contracts and agreements** – make sure they meet your organisation's requirements.

❑ **Be specific** – specify in contracts and agreements the standards, time, quantity, quality, control and consultation required.

❑ **Get good value** – check that the contract provides good value when compared with other suppliers.

❑ **Keep accurate records** – make sure contracts and agreements are fully documented, signed and kept available for reference.

❑ **Make sure contracts and agreements are legal, ethical and conform to the values and policies of the organisation** – check with specialists if you are in doubt.

Delegating authority to staff

❑ **Delegate responsibility and authority to competent staff –** only delegate to those capable of doing what is asked of them.

❑ **Be prepared to provide support where needed –** encourage staff to ask for support when required.

❑ **Delegate explicitly –** be clear and unambiguous about what is delegated and to whom.

❑ **Check understanding –** check that those to whom responsibility and authority has been delegated understand what is required of them, and confirm in writing, if necessary.

❑ **Delegate in time –** allow sufficient time for the action to be carried out.

❑ **Gain commitment –** delegate in a way which ensures understanding and inspires commitment and enthusiasm.

❑ **Agree the details –** agree with those concerned the way in which the responsibilities will be carried out and the resources available.

❑ **Provide sufficient resources –** make sure sufficient resources are readily available.

❑ **Provide equal opportunities –** provide equal opportunities to all staff to take on responsibilities.

❑ **Take advantage of diversity –** take advantage of the benefits of the diverse social, gender and racial mix of your staff in delegating authority.

❑ **Review delegation –** keep delegation under review and revise as necessary.

120 Agreeing targets

❑ **Agree clear targets** – only have targets which are necessary, unambiguous and explicit.

❑ **Agree targets with those responsible** – agree and, where appropriate, amend targets with those responsible for meeting them.

❑ **Take into account all relevant considerations** – when agreeing targets take into account the capabilities of the people concerned, the systems to be used and the circumstances which apply.

❑ **Make your targets consistent** – check that your targets are consistent with the objectives of your organisation and the details of operating plans.

❑ **Check the implications for other parts of your organisation** – where targets need to be revised, identify the implications for other parts of your organisation and communicate these to the relevant people.

❑ **Gain commitment** – agree and promote targets in ways which encourage creative thinking and commitment to these targets.

Providing advice and support

❏ **Provide advice and support to staff, contractors and suppliers**
– help them solve problems and maintain progress.

❏ **Provide advice and support at appropriate times and only when necessary** – do not interfere without good cause.

❏ **Provide advice and support in ways which**
  • confirm joint commitment to goals
  • demonstrate trust in those carrying out the work
  • give encouragement and reinforce confidence.

❏ **Be sensitive** – when providing advice and support, be sensitive to the personal needs and positions of those to whom you are offering it.

❏ **Enable individuals and groups to work autonomously** – only provide the advice and support necessary to allow them to make progress, then withdraw.

Championing activities

- ❑ **Promote benefits** – promote the benefits of programmes, projects and operations to stakeholders.
- ❑ **Identify threats** – identify threats to programmes, projects, operations and people at an early stage.
- ❑ **Counter threats** – where you can anticipate threats, take steps to counter them in the planning and delegation of work.
- ❑ **Consider the reasons and sources of threats** – take into account the reasons and sources of the threats in planning how to counter them.
- ❑ **Give clear support** – make your support apparent to those under threat and keep them regularly informed about the situation.

Culture

This section is about promoting a culture which is appropriate to your organisation's mission and values.

These checklists will help you to

- promote your organisation's values
- encourage collaboration between staff
- encourage a diversity of working styles and discourage rigid approaches.

This section covers

123 Promoting values in work

124 Encouraging collaboration

125 Encouraging diversity

123 **Promoting values in work**

❑ **Provide guidance** – be clear on the ways in which your organisation's values are to be expressed in work and in working relationships.

❑ **Consult with staff and other stakeholders** – consultation will help you gather ideas, suggestions and feedback on the ways in which values are expressed in work and in working relationships, as well as gaining commitment to those values.

❑ **Publish guidance on corporate values** – publish guidance to inform, explain and define the limits of acceptable practice.

❑ **Use appropriate means of consultation and guidance** – the means must suit the circumstances, degree of urgency and the likely reaction of the audience.

❑ **Be consistent** – make sure that the means of consultation and guidance are consistent with the policies and procedures of your organisation.

❑ **Commit to overcoming problems** – where problems occur which cannot be resolved in the normal way, be prepared to allocate additional resources to investigating and resolving them or to take disciplinary action where appropriate.

Encouraging collaboration

❏ **Explore collaborative and consultative working arrangements** – set these up where programmes, projects and operations would benefit from them.

❏ **Provide adequate resources** – provide the resources to allow collaborative and consultative working arrangements to succeed.

❏ **Induct and train participants** – help participants to understand the ways of working, backgrounds and expectations of their partners.

❏ **Be consistent** – ensure that targets, objectives, standards and values are consistent across the partners.

❏ **Provide support** – where difficulties in collaboration and consultation occur, provide support to help partners find ways to resolve them which remain consistent with your organisation's requirements.

125 Encouraging diversity

- ❏ **Encourage a diversity of working styles** – encourage teams and individuals to develop a repertoire of appropriate working styles.

- ❏ **Support natural working styles and behaviour** – encourage teams and individuals to use their natural and preferred working style and behaviour as long as they are consistent with the achievement of your organisation's objectives.

- ❏ **Discourage stereotyping** – discourage teams and individuals from imposing stereotypes and styles of working which are inconsistent with an individual's background.

- ❏ **Discourage rigid approaches** – where particular styles of working are inhibited without good work-related reasons, provide feedback and suggestions to encourage more diverse approaches.

- ❏ **Give feedback and suggestions sensitively** – where the style of working is inhibiting achievement of objectives, give feedback and suggestions to individuals in ways which are sensitive to their racial, social, gender or physical circumstances.

→ Control

This section is about developing a system to ensure you meet objectives and continue to improve your organisation's performance.

The checklists will help you to

- develop appropriate indicators to measure performance
- review the performance of projects and programmes against these indicators.

The process of **Control** looks like this.

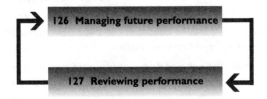

126 Managing future performance

127 Reviewing performance

Managing future performance

❏ **Propose and agree systems** – develop systems to help you manage future performance.

❏ **Draw on experience** – when designing systems for managing future performance, draw on your experience of current systems and on the ideas and advice of participants and experts.

❏ **Develop key indicators to control your organisation's performance** – develop key financial and other indicators to be able to monitor programmes, projects and plans.

❏ **Select realistic indicators** – select indicators, and the means of measuring them which are feasible, realistic and cost-effective.

❏ **Select timely indicators** – select indicators which will provide you with information in time to allow you to respond effectively.

❏ **Select reliable indicators** – select indicators which provide information to help you evaluate progress and predict future outcomes with a degree of certainty sufficient for decision-making.

❏ **Encourage participants to contribute** – develop systems which encourage participants to contribute to their own evaluation and allow for a diversity of contributions.

❏ **Identify the support needed** – ensure that systems identify the range of support required to enable performance targets to be met.

❏ **Explain systems clearly to all participants** – check their understanding and encourage them to ask for clarification.

❏ **Be ethical** – make sure your systems are ethical in concept and operation.

Reviewing performance

❑ **Obtain and evaluate data** – obtain and evaluate data on performance against your key indicators.

❑ **Evaluate in time** – evaluate your performance at a time and frequency which allows you to control progress and make an effective response.

❑ **Keep stakeholders informed** – evaluate your performance at a time and frequency which allows you to provide stakeholders with up-to-date plans.

❑ **Respond to contingencies** – evaluate your performance in a way which allows you to respond rapidly to contingencies or external factors.

❑ **Take differing views into account** – when evaluating your performance, take into account the views of those involved in the operations and resolve or report any differences of view.

❑ **Report potential problems** – report any potential problems in meeting performance targets to those who need to know in time for contingency action to be taken.

❑ **Be ethical** – ensure that you obtain data and evaluate it in an ethical manner.

CHAPTER 8

Evaluating and improving performance

Evaluating and improving performance is about checking that your organisation is on course for achieving its goals and finding ways of improving its performance in the future.

Evaluating and improving your organisation's performance

This section is about evaluating your organisation's performance in achieving its mission, objectives and policies and looking for ways to improve.

The checklists will help you to

- develop and evaluate your performance against appropriate measures and criteria
- identify why you have succeeded or failed
- consult with stakeholders about the findings
- reconsider your organisation's mission, objectives and policies in the light of these findings.

The process for *Evaluating and improving your organisation's performance* looks like this.

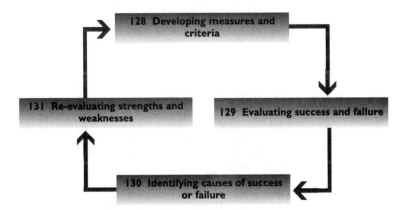

Developing measures and criteria

❑ **Develop techniques to evaluate your performance** – develop measures and criteria to evaluate the achievement of your organisation's mission, objectives and policies.

❑ **Select appropriate measures and criteria** – make sure they are appropriate to the nature and character of your mission, objectives and policies.

❑ **Use cost-effective measures and criteria** – make optimum use of existing sources of data and means of data gathering.

❑ **Get timely information** – choose measures and criteria which will provide you with information in time for you to respond effectively.

❑ **Get sufficient information to be able to make judgements** – choose measures and criteria which will give you sufficient information to make judgements about progress towards your mission and objectives and the implementation of your policies.

❑ **Take into account stakeholders' interests** – include the perspectives of your stakeholders in your measures and criteria.

Evaluating success and failure 129

❑ **Evaluate your organisation's performance** – evaluate the extent to which your organisation's mission, objectives and policies are being achieved.

❑ **Consider all the evidence** – both planned measures and informal sources of information.

❑ **Reach detailed conclusions based on clear criteria** – support these conclusions with facts.

❑ **Provide a rounded picture of your organisation's performance** – in respect of your mission, objectives and policies.

❑ **Discuss possible reasons for failure** – where performance fails to meet the agreed criteria, suggest possible reasons and discuss these with stakeholders.

❑ **Consult with stakeholders** – consult prior to the publication of any report on performance which may affect the interests of stakeholders.

❑ **Be fair and ethical** – make sure your evaluation is ethical, realistic and without favour to any groups or individuals.

130   Identifying causes of success or failure

❏ **Look for the causes of success or failure** – find out why the objectives of programmes, projects and operating plans are, or are not, being achieved.

❏ **Provide evidence** – support your explanations of the causes of success or failure with facts.

❏ **Evaluate your explanations** – estimate how likely it is that these are the real causes.

❏ **Explain your preferences** – where there are alternative explanations, report these and state the reason for your preference.

❏ **Present your arguments logically and comprehensively** – and summarise the arguments in ways which suit different audiences.

❏ **Prepare for objections** – where it is difficult to find a remedy for a cause, prepare your arguments to counter possible objections.

❏ **Learn from experience** – draw the lessons from success or failure, make these available to those who could learn from them and use them in your future planning.

❏ **Provide feedback to those whose performance is examined** – clearly explain the causes identified and encourage them to use this information to improve future performance.

Re-evaluating strengths and weaknesses

❑ **Re-evaluate your organisation –** consider the strengths and weaknesses of your organisation's mission, objectives and policies.

❑ **Reconsider evaluations of performance and achievement.**

❑ **Reconsider stakeholders' interests and views.**

❑ **Reconsider your organisation's vision and values.**

❑ **Reconsider trends in the external environment.**

❑ **Reconsider strengths and weaknesses in your internal assets.**

❑ **Provide a realistic and comprehensive analysis –** supported by evidence and arguments.

❑ **Make available your comments, analysis and recommendations –** so that these can be used for the review and reformulation of your mission, objectives and policies.

APPENDIX I

National standards

What are national standards?

National standards of performance, or occupational standards, have been developed for virtually all jobs in the UK today. The standards describe what people are expected to do in their jobs, and how they are expected to do them. There are occupational standards for retail staff, for cooks, care workers, administrative staff, construction workers and those in manufacturing and engineering industries, for instance.

The Management Standards, developed by the Management Charter Initiative (MCI), describe the standards of performance expected of managers and supervisors in their job role. They also describe the knowledge base which managers need in order to perform effectively. They apply to all managers and supervisors, regardless of the sector in which they are working. Whilst the context may be different, the process of, say, counselling staff, budgeting or implementing a change programme will be similar in all industries.

Organisations and managers in the private, public and voluntary sectors use the Management Standards for a wide range of purposes, including recruitment and selection, training needs analysis, design of training programmes, performance review and appraisal, succession planning and promotion criteria. Organisations are now beginning to link them to quality initiatives such as ISO9000, Total Quality Management and Investors in People.

However, the Management Standards, like all occupational standards, have been developed for assessment purposes, particularly assessment leading to National Vocational Qualifications (NVQs) or Scottish Vocational Qualifications (SVQs). Managers and supervisors can select those units of the Management Standards which are applicable to their role in order to be assessed for the following qualifications.

NVQ/SVQ Level 3 in Management	For managers and supervisors who have a tightly-defined area of responsibility with some limited opportunity for taking decisions and managing budgets. These managers are responsible for achieving specific results by using resources effectively and allocating work to members of their team, colleagues or contractors.
NVQ/SVQ Level 4 in Management	For managers who are responsible for allocating work to others and achieving specific results through the effective use of resources. These managers carry out policy in their defined area of authority and may have some limited responsibility for budgets. They contribute to broader activities, such as change programmes and recruitment, rather than having full responsibility for them.

NVQ/SVQ Level 5 in Operational Management	For managers who have operational responsibility for substantial programmes and resources. These managers have a broad span of control, they proactively identify and implement change and quality improvements, they negotiate budgets and contracts, and lead high-level meetings.
NVQ/SVQ Level 5 in Strategic Management	For managers who have responsibility for substantial programmes and resources and for the strategic development of their organisation. These managers have a broad span of control, they proactively identify and implement change and quality improvements, they negotiate budgets and contracts, and lead high-level meetings.

The checklists for Operational Management are relevant to all levels of management, although supervisors and first line managers may find they contribute to, rather than have full responsibility for, an activity.

The section on Operational Management is based mainly on the NVQ/SVQ Level 5 in Operational Management and on other appropriate standards, such as those developed by the Accounting Lead Body, the Commercial Occupational Standards Council and the Employment Occupational Standards Council (addresses in Appendix 2).

The section in this guide on Strategic Management is based largely on the NVQ/SVQ Level 5 in Strategic Management.

The links between the checklists and the integrated structure of the Management Standards are shown on pages 218-221.

National Vocational Qualifications

National Vocational Qualifications (NVQs), and Scottish Vocational Qualifications (SVQs), are certificates of employees' competence in the job-role. They are available to anyone who can prove that they are competent in all the units of the appropriate set of occupational standards.

There are five levels in the NVQ framework. Retail staff, for instance, can gain NVQs in retailing at level 1-4, carpenters at level 2 or 3 and telesales staff at level 2.

The NVQ Framework

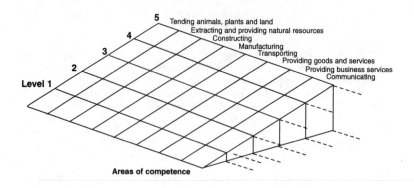

5 Tending animals, plants and land
Extracting and providing natural resources
Constructing
Manufacturing
Transporting
Providing goods and services
Providing business services
Communicating

Level 1

Areas of competence

Regardless of the sector of the economy you are working in, you can be awarded an NVQ or SVQ at level 3, 4 or 5 in management, if you can satisfy an assessor that you are competent in the Management Standards at the appropriate level.

You will usually need to compile a portfolio of evidence supporting your claim to competence and submit this to an assessor at an Approved Centre. An NVQ or SVQ is not a training programme. It is a certificate of your competence to do your job as a manager. Of course, you may need some training or development to attain that level of competence.

If you are interested in gaining an NVQ or SVQ, contact your local Approved Centre, details are available from the Management Charter Initiative (address in Appendix 2).

The NVQ process

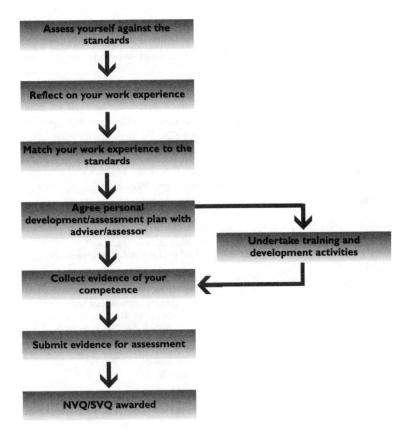

Assess yourself against the standards

↓

Reflect on your work experience

↓

Match your work experience to the standards

↓

Agree personal development/assessment plan with adviser/assessor

Undertake training and development activities

↓

Collect evidence of your competence

↓

Submit evidence for assessment

↓

NVQ/SVQ awarded

The integrated structure of management standards

The new integrated structure of Management Standards, launched in 1997, describes all the functions of management which one would expect to see performed within an organisation. One would not expect to see any one manager carrying out all these functions.

Managers can use the integrated structure to identify those units and elements from the Management Standards which best describe their job role. Organisations can use the integrated structure to audit their management competence, identify who does what and plan for organisational development to improve management structures and communication systems.

The integrated structure draws together the seven key roles of management: Manage Activities, Manage Resources, Manage People, Manage Information, Manage Energy, Manage Quality and Manage Projects.

Manage activities	This key role describes the manager's work in managing the operation to meet customers' requirements and continuously improve performance.
Manage resources	This key role describes the manager's work in planning and using physical resources effectively and efficiently. Physical resources include money, premises, capital equipment, energy, supplies and materials. They do not include people or information which are dealt with under separate key roles.
Manage people	This key role describes the work of all managers in getting the most from their teams. It does not, however, cover specialist personnel management issues. It covers recruiting, training, building the team, allocating and evaluating work, and dealing with people problems. It also includes managing yourself and relations with others at work.
Manage information	This key role describes the manager's role in obtaining, analysing and using information effectively and also covers leading and contributing to meetings.
Manage energy	This key role describes the work of those managers with special responsibility for ensuring the organisation develops and implements policies for using energy in the most efficient way.
Manage quality	Continuous improvement and quality are responsibilities of all managers and are themes running throughout the Management Standards. The key role *Manage Quality* describes the specialist responsibilities of the quality manager, covering total quality management, quality assurance and quality control.
Manage projects	This key role describes the work of those responsible for planning, controlling and completing projects to the client's satisfaction.

Manage activities

Unit	Elements
A1 Maintain activities to meet requirements	A1.1 Maintain work activities to meet requirements A1.2 Maintain healthy, safe and productive work conditions A1.3 Make recommendations for improvements to work activities
A2 Manage activities to meet requirements	A2.1 Implement plans to meet customer requirements A2.2 Maintain a healthy, safe and productive work environment A2.3 Ensure products and services meet quality requirements
A3 Manage activities to meet customer requirements	A3.1 Agree customer requirements A3.2 Plan activities to meet customer requirements A3.3 Provide a healthy, safe and productive work environment A3.4 Ensure products and services meet customer requirements
A4 Contribute to improvements at work	A4.1 Improve work activities A4.2 Recommend improvements to organisational plans
A5 Manage change in organisational activities	A5.1 Identify opportunities for improvements in activities A5.2 Evaluate proposed changes for benefits and disadvantages A5.3 Plan the implementation of change in activities A5.4 Agree the introduction of change A5.5 Implement changes in activities
A6 Review external and internal operating environments	A6.1 Analyse your organisation's external operating environment A6.2 Evaluate competitors and collaborators A6.3 Develop effective relationships with stakeholders A6.4 Review your organisation's structures and systems

Manage activities (continued)

Unit	Elements
A7 Establish strategies to guide the work of your organisation	A7.1 Create a shared vision and mission to give purpose to your organisation A7.2 Define values and policies to guide the work of your organisation A7.3 Formulate objectives and strategies to guide your organisation A7.4 Gain support for organisational strategies
A8 Evaluate and improve organisational performance	A8.1 Develop measures and criteria to evaluate your organisation's performance A8.2 Evaluate your organisation's performance A8.3 Explain the causes of success and failure in organisational strategies

Manage resources

Unit	Elements
B1 Support the efficient use of resources	B1.1 Make recommendations for the use of resources B1.2 Contribute to the control of resources
B2 Manage the use of physical resources	B2.1 Plan the use of physical resources B2.2 Obtain physical resources B2.3 Ensure availability of supplies B2.4 Monitor the use of physical resources
B3 Manage the use of financial resources	B3.1 Make recommendations for expenditure B3.2 Control expenditure against budgets
B4 Determine the effective use of resources	B4.1 Make proposals for expenditure on programmes of work B4.2 Agree budgets for programmes of work B4.3 Control expenditure and activities against budgets
B5 Secure financial resources for your organisation's plans	B5.1 Review the generation and allocation of financial resources B5.2 Evaluate proposals for expenditure B5.3 Obtain financial resources for your organisation's activities

Manage people

Unit	Elements
C1 Manage yourself	C1.1 Develop your own skills to improve your performance C1.2 Manage your time to meet your objectives
C2 Develop your own resources	C2.1 Develop yourself to improve your performance C2.2 Manage your own time and resources to meet your objectives
C3 Enhance your own performance	C3.1 Continuously develop your own knowledge and skills C3.2 Optimise your own resources to meet your objectives
C4 Create effective working relationships	C4.1 Gain the trust and support of colleagues and team members C4.2 Gain the trust and support of your manager C4.3 Minimise conflict in your team
C5 Develop productive working relationships	C5.1 Develop the trust and support of colleagues and team members C5.2 Develop the trust and support of your manager C5.3 Minimise interpersonal conflict
C6 Enhance productive working relationships	C6.1 Enhance the trust and support of colleagues C6.2 Enhance the trust and support of those to whom you report C6.3 Provide guidance on values at work
C7 Contribute to the selection of personnel for activities	C7.1 Contribute to the identifying personnel requirements C7.2 Contribute to selecting required personnel
C8 Select personnel for activities	C8.1 Identify personnel requirements C8.2 Select required personnel

Manage people (continued)

Unit	Elements
C9 Contribute to the development of teams and individuals	C9.1 Contribute to the identification of development needs C9.2 Contribute to planning development of teams and individuals C9.3 Contribute to development activities C9.4 Contribute to assessment of people against development objectives
C10 Develop teams and individuals to enhance performance	C10.1 Identify the development needs of teams and individuals C10.2 Plan the development of teams and individuals C10.3 Develop teams to improve performance C10.4 Support individual learning and development C10.5 Assess the development of teams and individuals C10.6 Improve the development of teams and individuals
C11 Develop management teams	C11.1 Assess the effectiveness of management teams C11.2 Improve the effectiveness of management teams
C12 Lead the work of teams and individuals to achieve their objectives	C12.1 Plan the work of teams and individuals C12.2 Assess the work of teams and individuals C12.3 Provide feedback to teams and individuals on their work
C13 Manage the performance of teams and individuals	C13.1 Allocate work to teams and individuals C13.2 Agree objectives and work plans with teams and individuals C13.3 Assess the performance of teams and individuals C13.4 Provide feedback to teams and individuals on their performance
C14 Delegate work to others	C14.1 Delegate responsibility and authority to others C14.2 Agree targets for delegated work C14.3 Provide advice and support for delegated work C14.4 Promote and protect delegated work and those who carry it out

Manage people (continued)

Unit	Elements
C15 Respond to poor performance in your team	C15.1 Help team members who have problems affecting their performance C15.2 Contribute to implementing disciplinary and grievance procedures
C16 Deal with poor performance in your team	C16.1 Support team members who have problems affecting their performance C16.2 Implement disciplinary and grievance procedures C16.3 Dismiss team members whose performance is unsatisfactory
C17 Redeploy personnel and make redundancies	C17.1 Plan the redeployment of personnel C17.2 Redeploy personnel C17.3 Make personnel redundant

Manage information

Unit	Elements
D1 Manage information for action	D1.1 Gather required information D1.2 Inform and advise others D1.3 Hold meetings
D2 Facilitate meetings	D2.1 Lead meetings D2.2 Make contributions to meetings
D3 Chair and participate in meetings	D3.1 Chair meetings D3.2 Participate in meetings
D4 Provide information to support decision-making	D4.1 Obtain information for decision-making D4.2 Record and store information D4.3 Analyse information to support decision-making D4.4 Advise and inform others
D5 Establish information management and communication systems	D5.1 Identify information and communication requirements D5.2 Select information management and communication systems D5.3 Implement information management and communication systems D5.4 Monitor information management and communication systems
D6 Use information to take critical decisions	D6.1 Obtain information needed to take critical decisions D6.2 Analyse information for decision-making D6.3 Take critical decisions D6.4 Advise and inform others

Manage energy

Unit	Elements
E1 Identify the scope for improvement in the way the organisation manages energy	E1.1 Audit the organisation's performance in the way it manages energy E1.2 Identify improvements to the way the organisation manages energy
E2 Provide advice on the development and implementation of energy policies	E2.1 Provide advice on the development of policies for the use of energy E2.2 Recommend strategies to implement energy policies
E3 Promote energy efficiency	E3.1 Promote energy efficiency throughout the organisation E3.2 Promote the organisation's achievements in energy efficiency
E4 Monitor and evaluate energy efficiency	E4.1 Establish systems and processes to monitor and evaluate energy usage E4.2 Obtain, analyse and record information on energy efficiency performance E4.3 Evaluate the organisation's energy efficiency performance
E5 Identify improvements to energy efficiency	E5.1 Identify opportunities to improve energy efficiency E5.2 Recommend improvements to energy efficiency
E6 Provide advice and support for the development of energy efficient practices	E6.1 Support the development of a culture of energy awareness E6.2 Provide advice and support for energy efficient practices
E7 Provide advice and support for the development and implementation of systems to measure energy usage	E7.1 Provide support for the development of systems to measure energy usage E7.2 Provide support for the collection, analysis and recording of information on energy usage E7.3 Provide advice on trends and developments in energy usage

Manage energy (continued)

Unit	Elements
E8 Provide advice and support for improving energy efficiency	E8.1 Encourage involvement in energy efficiency activities
	E8.2 Provide advice on the competences needed to use energy efficiently
	E8.3 Provide advice on the training needed to use energy efficiently
E9 Determine conditions in the market for supplies	E9.1 Establish the organisation's position in the marketplace
	E9.2 Identify market changes likely to affect supplies
	E9.3 Determine the competitiveness of supplies from the market
	E9.4 Identify beneficial developments relating to supplies and sources.

Manage quality

Unit	Elements
F1 Promote the importance and benefits of quality	F1.1 Promote the importance of quality in the organisation's strategy F1.2 Promote quality throughout the organisation and its customer and supplier networks
F2 Provide advice and support for the development and implementation of quality policies	F2.1 Provide advice and support for the development of quality policies F2.2 Provide advice and support for the development of strategies to implement quality policies
F3 Manage continuous quality improvement	F3.1 Develop and implement systems to monitor and evaluate organisational performance F3.2 Promote continuous quality improvement for products, services and processes
F4 Implement quality assurance systems	F4.1 Establish quality assurance systems F4.2 Maintain quality assurance systems F4.3 Recommend improvements to quality assurance systems
F5 Provide advice and support for the development and implementation of quality systems	F5.1 Provide advice and support for the assessment of processes and working environments F5.2 Provide advice and support for the development of plans to improve quality systems F5.3 Provide advice and support for the development of measurement systems F5.4 Provide advice and support for the collection, analysis and documentation of information
F6 Monitor compliance with quality systems	F6.1 Plan to audit compliance with quality systems F6.2 Implement the audit plan F6.3 Report on compliance with quality systems
F7 Carry out quality audits	F7.1 Audit compliance with quality systems F7.2 Follow up quality audits

Manage projects

Unit	Elements
G1 Contribute to project planning and preparation	G1.1 Clarify the project's scope and definition G1.2 Provide plans to achieve the project's goals G1.3 Contribute to project preparation
G2 Coordinate the running of projects	G2.1 Support the project team G2.2 Coordinate activities, resources and plans G2.3 Keep stakeholders informed of project progress
G3 Contribute to project closure	G3.1 Complete project activities G3.2 Contribute to the evaluation of project planning and implementation
G4 Plan and prepare projects	G4.1 Agree the project's scope and definition with the sponsor G4.2 Develop plans to achieve the project's goals G4.3 Establish the project's resourcing and control methods
G5 Manage the running of projects	G5.1 Lead the project team G5.2 Monitor and adjust activities, resources and plans G5.3 Develop solutions to project problems G5.4 Maintain communication with project stakeholders
G6 Complete projects	G6.1 Ensure the completion of project activities G6.2 Evaluate the effectiveness of project planning and implementation

Links between the checklists and the management standards

Operational management checklists	Elements of management standards
Meeting customer needs	
1 Agreeing customer requirements	A3.1
2 Planning to meet customer requirements	A2.1, A3.2
3 Maintaining supplies	B2.3
4 Maintaining a productive work environment	A1.2, A2.2, A3.3
5 Meeting customer specifications	A1.1, A2.3, A3.4
6 Solving problems for customers	A3.4
Marketing	
7 Developing your markets	
8 Developing a marketing plan	
9 Developing new products and services	Marketing Standards (refer to COSC: Appendix 2)
10 Determining a pricing strategy	
11 Deciding on distribution methods	
12 Developing a communications plan	
13 Developing a sales strategy	
14 Evaluating marketing activity	
Managing change	
15 Identifying opportunities for improvements	A1.3, A4.1-2, A5.1
16 Assessing the pros and cons of change	A5.2
17 Planning change	A5.3
18 Negotiating and agreeing the introduction of change	A5.4
19 Implementing and evaluating changes	A5.5
Project management	
20 Agreeing project scope	G1.1, G4.1
21 Developing project plans	G1.2, G4.2
22 Securing required resources	G1.3, G4.3
23 Controlling project activities	G2.1-3, G5.1-3
24 Closing out projects	G3.1-2, G6.1-3
Quality assurance	
25 Establishing quality assurance systems	F4.1
26 Implementing and maintaining quality assurance systems	F4.2
27 Improving quality assurance systems	F4.3
Environmental management	
28 Identifying environmental responsibilities	
29 Assessing environmental impact	
30 Reviewing environmental performance	Environmental Management Standards (under development by MCI)
31 Establishing an environmental management policy	
32 Implementing an environmental management system	
33 Dealing with emergencies	
34 Auditing environmental performance	
35 Promoting environmental awareness	

What are national standards?

Operational management checklists	Elements of management standards
Managing yourself	
36 Managing your time	C1.2, C2.2, C3.2
37 Developing your skills	C1.1, C2.1, C3.1
Personnel planning	
38 Planning human resource requirements	C7.1, C8.1
39 Drawing up job specifications	C7.1, C8.1
40 Attracting the right candidates	—
41 Assessing and selecting team members	C7.2, C8.2
42 Appointing team members	—
43 Inducting new team members	—
44 Redeploying people	C17.1, C17.2
45 Making people redundant	C17.3
Developing teams and individuals	
46 Developing teams	C9.1-3, C10.1-3
47 Developing individuals	C10.4
48 Coaching	C10.4
49 Mentoring	C10.4
50 Assessing teams and individuals	C9.4, C10.5
51 Evaluating and improving training and development	C10.6
Managing teams and individuals	
52 Planning work	C12.1
53 Allocating work	C13.1
54 Agreeing objectives	C13.2
55 Reviewing performance	C12.2, C13.3
56 Giving feedback	C12.3, C13.4
Working relationships	
57 Building a good reporting relationship	C4.2, C5.2, C6.2
58 Building relationships with your team	C4.1, C5.1, C6.1
59 Building relationships with colleagues	C4.1, C5.1, C6.1
60 Minimising conflict	C4.3, C5.3
Managing problems with your team	
61 Counselling	C15.1, C16.1
62 Implementing grievance and disciplinary procedures	C15.2, C16.2
63 Dismissing people	C16.3
Equal opportunities	
64 Promoting equal opportunities	—
65 Encouraging diversity and fair working practices	—
Managing physical resources	
66 Securing physical resources	B1.1, B2.1-2
67 Using physical resources effectively	B1.2, B2.4

Operational management checklists	Elements of management standards

Managing budgets

68	Preparing budgets	B3.1, B4.1
69	Negotiating and agreeing budgets	B4.2
70	Monitoring budgets	B3.2, B4.3

Controlling finances

71	Controlling costs	B1.2, B3.2, B4.3
72	Managing cash flow	Accounting
73	Credit control	Standards

Selecting suppliers

74	Selecting potential suppliers	Purchasing &
75	Obtaining bids	Supply Standards
76	Obtaining tenders	(refer to
77	Clarifying and improving offers	COSC:
78	Deciding on supplier	Appendix 2)

Contracting for supply

79	Negotiating supply agreements	Purchasing &
80	Establishing a contract for supply	Supply Standards
81	Placing a contract for supply	(refer to
82	Dealing with contractual problems	COSC:
83	Resolving problems in supply	Appendix 2)

Managing energy

84	Assessing energy performance	E1.1, E4.1-3
85	Developing energy efficient plans and practices	E2.1-2, E6.1-2
86	Continuously improving energy efficiency	E5.1-2, E8.1-3.

Establishing information management and communication systems

87	Identifying information and communication requirements	D5.1
88	Selecting information management and communication systems	D5.2
89	Implementing information management and communication systems	D5.3
90	Monitoring information management and communication systems	D5.4

Using information

91	Obtaining and evaluating information	D1.1, D4.1, D6.1
92	Recording and storing information	D1.1, D4.2
93	Analysing information	D4.3, D6.2
94	Forecasting trends and developments	D4.3, D6.2
95	Taking critical decisions	D6.3
96	Presenting information and advice	D1.2, D4.4, D6.4

Meetings

97	Leading meetings	D1.3, D2.1, D3.1
98	Participating in meetings	D2.2, D3.2

What are national standards?

Strategic management checklists	Elements of management standards
Reviewing the external environment	
99 Researching your markets	A6.1
100 Responding to the political and trading environment	A6.1
101 Identifying competitors and partners	A6.2
Reviewing your organisation	
102 Reviewing your products and services	—
103 Reviewing your organisational structures	A6.4
104 Reviewing management capability	C11.1
105 Developing your management team	C11.2
106 Reviewing your financial resources	B5.1
Stakeholders	
107 Identifying stakeholders' interests	A6.3
108 Getting the best from stakeholders	A6.3
Agreeing your strategy	
109 Defining your organisation's vision and mission	A7.1
110 Defining your organisation's values and policies	A7.2
111 Defining your organisation's objectives	A7.3
112 Gaining support for your strategy	A7.4
Developing programmes, projects and plans	
113 Submitting proposals	B4.1
114 Evaluating and amending proposals	B5.2
115 Providing professional or technical advice	B5.2
116 Generating support and securing resources	B5.3
117 Gaining agreement for your plans	B4.2
Delegating and taking action	
118 Negotiating contracts with suppliers	B2.3
119 Delegating authority to staff	C14.1
120 Agreeing targets	C14.2
121 Providing advice and support	C14.3
122 Championing activities	C14.4
Culture	
123 Promoting values in work	C6.3
124 Encouraging collaboration	—
125 Encouraging diversity	—
Control	
126 Managing future performance	C13.3
127 Reviewing performance	C13.4
Evaluating and improving your organisation's performance	
128 Developing measures and criteria	A8.1
129 Evaluating success and failure	A8.2
130 Identifying causes of success or failure	A8.3
131 Re-evaluating strengths and weaknesses	A8.3

APPENDIX 2

Useful addresses

The following organisations are referred to in the text.

Accounting Lead Body
154 Clerkenwell Road
London EC1R 5AD

Tel: 0171 837 8600
Fax: 0171 837 6970

Commercial Occupational Standards Council
The Brackens
London Road
Ascot
Berkshire SL5 8BJ

Tel: 01344 886244
Fax: 01344 886266

Employment Occupational Standards Council
Room 32
4th Floor, Kimberley House
47 Vaughan Way
Leicester LE1 4ST

Tel: 0116 251 7979
Fax: 0116 251 1464

Management Charter Initiative
Russell Square House
10-12 Russell Square
London WC1B 5BZ

Tel: 0171 872 9000
Fax: 0171 872 9099

Scottish Qualifications Authority (formerly SCOTVEC)
Hanover House
24 Douglas Street
Glasgow G2 7NQ

Tel: 0141 248 7900
Fax: 0141 242 2244

Qualifications and Curriculum Authority (formerly NCVQ)
222 Euston Road
London NW1 2BZ

Tel: 0171 387 9898
Fax: 0171 387 0978

Index

Index